Ernest J. Oppenheimer

THE
INFLATION
SWINDLE

ERNEST J. OPPENHEIMER, Ph.D.

PRENTICE-HALL, INC., ENGLEWOOD CLIFFS, N. J.

The Inflation Swindle
by Ernest J. Oppenheimer, Ph.D.
Copyright © 1977 by Ernest J. Oppenheimer

Printed in the United States of America

Prentice-Hall International, Inc., London
Prentice-Hall of Australia, Pty. Ltd., Sydney
Prentice-Hall of Canada, Ltd., Toronto
Prentice-Hall of India Private Ltd., New Delhi
Prentice-Hall of Japan, Inc., Tokyo
Prentice-Hall of Southeast Asia Pte. Ltd., Singapore
Whitehall Books Limited, Wellington, New Zealand

10 9 8 7 6 5 4 3 2 1

Library of Congress Cataloging in Publication Data

Oppenheimer, Ernest J.
    The inflation swindle.

    1.   Inflation (Finance)—United States. I. Title.
HG538.O67   332.4'1'0973   77-4067
ISBN 0-13-464420-4

CONTENTS

PREFACE

Inflation is a problem that has many ramifications. Its most apparent effects are in the financial sphere, for it is clearly a distortion of the monetary function. Because money is used in the structuring and measuring of economic activities, inflation is of significance to economists. The federal government plays the key role in causing inflation; therefore, an understanding of governmental and political processes is essential. The evidence is strong that inflation violates constitutional provisions safeguarding property from governmental expropriation without due process of law. Consequently, there are important legal and judicial ramifications. Last but not least, inflation raises profound moral questions, for it rewards those who chronically live beyond their means at the expense of those who try to take care of their own needs by prudence and the accumulation of savings. In effect, inflation causes a massive undermining of ethical precepts.

It is evident from the above that the ideal combination of skills for studying inflation would consist of expertise in finance, economics, political science, constitutional law, and ethics. While it is virtually impossible for anyone to be an expert in all these fields, it is essential that the problem be dealt with in terms of these realities. Insofar as any of these dimensions are ignored, we will lack the proper perspective for understanding and controlling inflation.

My background includes some fifteen years of practical experience in the field of finance, about three years employment by the U.S. government, and a doctor of philosophy degree in international relations. The latter involved studies in political science, economics, diplomacy, international law, and other fields. My family suffered destruction of property through the inflation in Germany of the 1920s. All of these experiences have played a role in providing me with the motivations and qualifications for writing a book about inflation.

I started the formal investigation of inflation toward the end of 1970. The rate of inflation at that time was approximately 6 percent. When wage and price controls were instituted in the summer of 1971, my contacts in Washington were convinced that this would bring about the end of inflation. I did not share their optimism. While the rate of inflation declined to around 3 percent by 1972, it reached 11 percent two years later. The large federal deficits incurred in 1971–73 provided a good indication that more inflation was just around the corner. A similar, but much more ominous, situation confronts us over the next several years. We have just passed through the most severe recession since the 1930s. The government has incurred unprecedented deficits with built-in inflation-producing potential. If we do not take appropriate measures, such as those advanced in the last part of this book, our monetary system is in serious jeopardy.

The objective of this book is to make the realities of inflation understandable to as wide a segment of the American public as possible. This is necessary in order to mobilize public opinion against the dangers to our society. While the subject matter is inherently somewhat complicated, I have attempted to explain the facts in language that the average reader can understand. Where technical terms are used, they are either explained in the text or defined in the Glossary. In order to get optimum use from the Glossary, it may be helpful to the reader to glance at it as soon as possible.

INTRODUCTION

Dictionaries tend to define inflation in terms of abnormal increases in money and credit which result in rising general price levels. These definitions do not explain who causes inflation or for what purposes. Adam Smith, the father of free enterprise economic theory, takes care of this deficiency by noting that throughout history governments heavily in debt have used their control over the currency to change the rules in favor of debtors. In early times, this was done by debasing the coin. The procedure was to add ordinary metals to the precious ones, with the stated value of the coin remaining unchanged. For example, a coin containing $10 worth of gold was replaced by one whose gold content was $5, with the balance consisting of some worthless substance. This enabled the government to issue twice as many coins as previously, and thus doubled general price levels. The ruler decreed that the new coins had the same value as the old ones. The effect of this procedure was to wipe out half of all outstanding debts, notably those of the government itself. Adam Smith labeled this action "a disguised form of bankruptcy," which defrauded all creditors. The people tried to protect their interests by hoarding the genuine gold pieces and by using only the debased coins for payments. This reality was formulated into an economic law by the sixteenth-century English financier Sir Thomas Gresham, who noted that bad money drives good money out of circulation.

Modern governments are more adept at this game and have made it virtually impossible for the people to protect themselves against currency manipulations. In most countries today almost all money is created by fiat and has no intrinsic value. This fact gives the governments an almost free hand to exploit their citizens at will. Moreover, the procedures used are so esoteric that the average person has no chance to comprehend what is going on, much less to protect himself against it. For example, in the United States the Federal Reserve converts government debts into new reserve assets of the banking system, using fiat money to pay for its purchases. In this fashion, since 1940 the Federal Reserve has acquired some $100 billion of government securities, effectively reducing the government's debt by that amount. In addition, it has infused an estimated $700 billion of new funds into the banking system, thus undermining all existing monetary values by means of inflation. Removing the clever disguises, we find that the U.S. government has created new money by a stroke of the pen, has used that fiat money to reduce its indebtedness outright (by the purchase of government securities), and has utilized its control over the banking system to generate a multiplication of these funds. This procedure makes inflation inevitable, which further benefits the government by reducing the purchasing power of its outstanding debt. The old kings were mere blunderers in comparison with the experts running our financial affairs today.

In terms of its impact on society, the chronic inflation of the past four decades is the biggest swindle in

American history. During this period savers, taxpayers, and creditors have suffered losses of purchasing power amounting to hundreds of billions of dollars. The rules of finance have been turned upside down to benefit the profligate spenders and dissipaters of wealth at the expense of the prudent accumulators of savings. All the realities and lessons of history have been overlooked in the process. If appropriate measures to conquer inflation are not taken in time, the very existence of our society is in jeopardy.

The biggest victim of inflation is money itself. Money is supposed to fulfill the functions of medium of exchange, standard of value for long-term transactions, and store of value for savings. These functions require stability in the purchasing power of money over time. Chronic inflation is antithetical to stability. Since money is the cement that holds the economy and society together, inflation constitutes a grave threat to the viability of our most basic institutions.

Inflation is the inevitable result of self-serving government policies that endeavor to control the economy through financial manipulations. Ever since the New Deal days, the U.S. government has tried to stimulate economic activity by the infusion of fiat funds and the resultant low interest rates. The objectives of this financial strategy were to safeguard the economy against declines and to assure full employment. As events have shown, neither of these objectives was achieved. Recessions of increasing severity have hit the economy and unemployment has reached the highest levels since the 1930s. While the ostensible purposes of the financial manipulations were unfulfilled, other consequences became increasingly apparent. The federal government, as the largest single borrower, was the major beneficiary of the fiat money stream. It could engage in chronic deficit financing without worrying about financial discipline; it was able to borrow funds at interest rates below inflation rates plus a normal return on capital (see Chapter 4); it could repay maturing debts with depreciated currency; and it increased its income tax receipts through inflation's impact on graduated, escalating tax rates (see Chapter 5).

It is apparent that whatever lofty intentions those in government might have expressed in relation to the economy, the actual events show that the infusion of fiat funds was of primary benefit to the government, not to the economy. In fact, there is convincing evidence that the whole financial manipulation was counterproductive for the economy. Debts have accumulated at an alarming pace, force-fed by Federal Reserve easy money policies. Such debts exceeded $3 trillion (three thousand billion dollars) by the end of 1975. (*U.S. News & World Report*, November 17, 1975). Normal business decisions have been complicated by inflationary realities. Financial markets have been weakened. Discipline and morale of all participants in the economic process have been undermined. Economic cooperation for the benefit of all has been increasingly replaced by ruthlessly exploitative behavior. The effects of inflation have many of the characteristics of financial neurosis.

Adam Smith's thesis that governments are the culprits in causing inflation through currency manipulations in order to escape debt obligations and financial discipline is irrefutable. What we have witnessed in the United States during the past four decades is a modern variation on that theme. At the core of the government's financial manipulations is the reality that Washington has become increasingly overextended, with budgets virtually out of control, deficits on an unprecedented scale, and debts mushrooming to new heights year after year. If this sequence of events took place with a private individual or corporation, it would long ago have resulted in either a sharp retrenchment or open bankruptcy. The government avoids this condition by manipulating the currency in such a way that the burden of its profligacy is passed on to the people. Inflation is, in effect, a technique for converting the government's bankruptcy into the people's problem. It is a far more insidious and damaging procedure than open bankruptcy, for it victimizes everybody and knows no limits.

There is strong evidence that the government's procedures violate constitutional provisions against depriving people of their property without due process of law. The government has partially substituted self-serving financial manipulations for legitimate tax policies. Inflation poses serious threats to the very essence of democracy.

Inflation can be conquered by reversing the trends that have characterized government policies since the 1930s. The benefits derived from inflation by the government must be removed. New government debt issues should be inflation-proofed by linking them to the cost-of-living index. Interest rate manipulations for the benefit of borrowers must be stopped. The deceptive procedure of converting government debt into new reserve assets of the banking system, financed with fiat money, should be replaced with a mechanism whose sole purpose is the maintenance of stable prices. Income taxes should be adjusted for inflation rates. The government should learn to live within its means and rely on taxes openly arrived at for its income, not on deceptive manipulations of the currency.

By concentrating on putting its own financial house in order, the government will of course have to reduce its role in regulating the economy. This will be all to the good, for the government has clearly failed in its endeavors to prevent recessions and unemployment, and may indeed have added to these problems. The biggest contribution that the government can make to economic soundness is to work wholeheartedly on putting an end to the inflation swindle.

While the main focus of this book is on the federal government's role in relation to inflation, the impact on individuals, corporations, and local governments is also given consideration. Within the framework of a disguised form of national bankruptcy, the best one can attempt to do is to reduce exposure and minimize losses. Experience has

shown that virtually all attempts to profit from inflation
entail considerable risks and ultimately may prove to be
self-defeating. Inflation is basically a political and moral
problem and ought to be dealt with primarily on those
levels. It is hoped that this book will supply the reader with
the information necessary to enable him or her to take an
active and intelligent part in the fight against inflation.

TWO CLASSICAL PERSPECTIVES

Adam Smith noted that throughout history governments have used their control over the currency to defraud their creditors. He called this procedure a "disguised form of bankruptcy." This is a succinct explanation of what happens under chronic inflationary conditions. Alfred Marshall, one of the outstanding economic theorists of the nineteenth century, pioneered the concept of "purchasing power units" to prevent abuse of the monetary system. This approach has direct applicability to the inflationary environment.

The term "inflation" was only invented during the American Civil War, but the governmental practice of undermining the currency's purchasing power to avoid paying creditors in full is very old indeed. Adam Smith was fully cognizant of this reality. As he analyzed economic history, he found that the process which culminates in "disguised bankruptcy" always starts with governments living beyond their means, usually as a result of wars. Under these conditions, they borrowed large sums. Invariably, the government's profligate habits are copied by others and soon an increasing number of people are living beyond their means. This constituency of borrowers then joins with the government in urging that the currency be undermined, enabling them to pay back only a portion of what they owe in real terms. This process shifts wealth from the industrious and frugal to the profligate spenders and dissipaters of capital. Thus, the relationship between lenders and borrowers is the key to understanding inflation.

As an early example Adam Smith cites the Roman Republic, which manipulated the *as*, their monetary unit, to finance the costs of the wars with Carthage. Having borrowed heavily from its citizens, and being unable to repay them in full, the Roman government resorted to currency devaluation. In two steps, the copper content of the *as*, which originally was twelve ounces, was reduced to half an ounce. In this way the government wiped out over 95 percent of its indebtedness, conveniently forgetting the fact that this procedure also eliminated most of the savings of its citizens. The latter soon thereafter overthrew their government.

Adam Smith emphasized that this Roman experience is not an exception, but is the normal sequence of events in the dealings of governments with their creditors. He noted that the history of government indebtedness makes sad reading. He could not find a single instance of a major government debt being fully and fairly repaid without loss of purchasing power to the creditors. The two hundred years that have elapsed since Smith wrote his *Wealth of Nations* have served to substantiate the essential correctness of his observations.

It is noteworthy that Adam Smith made these comments at a time when money was primarily in the form of gold or other precious metals. Thus, inflation is not prevented by gold currencies, for governments in debt find ways of manipulating the content or price of gold if they cannot get their way via the printing press. The key fact to keep in mind is that large government debts invariably lead to policies of "disguised bankruptcy," no matter what the nature of the currency. If governments had no incentive to reduce the value of money, the latter would remain stable regardless of its form. Contrariwise, if there is a strong incentive to reduce indebtedness by cheapening currencies, ways and means will be found to accomplish this.

Adam Smith was not optimistic about the outlook for a nation's currency as long as the government was heavily in debt. If such debts were incurred as a result of a major emergency, such as a war, he felt that they should be paid off as soon as possible. To encourage governments to incur debts for economic purposes—a procedure recommended by the British economist John Maynard Keynes—would have been considered folly and charlatanism by Smith. The latter knew governments too well to give them such powers. History has proved him right.

The great value of Smith's orientation is its clarity and profundity. He went right to the heart of the matter and was not diverted by either confused thinking or weak terminology. The word *inflation*, having a neutral connotation, lends itself to rationalizations which are exposed as sham by Adam Smith. For example, those who believe that a "little inflation" may be helpful in stimulating economic activity would have a much harder time getting their notions across if they had to say that a "little bankruptcy" is a good thing. Adam Smith believed in calling a spade a spade, a quality which we might do well to emulate if we want to come to grips with the problem of inflation.

The second classical perspective on inflation is provided by Alfred Marshall. The source for his views is the chapter entitled "Remedies for Fluctuations of General Prices," which appeared in *Memorials of Alfred Marshall* (edited by A. C. Pigou, published in London by MacMillan & Co., Ltd. in 1925). Marshall showed how a fundamental misconception about the functions of money is a major cause of financial instability, including inflation. Historically, the role of money was largely confined to that of medium of exchange for instantaneously completed transactions. For example, most goods and services were sold and paid for immediately. Transactions involving delay between performance and payments were relatively rare. This situation changed drastically in the nineteenth century. As a result of the Industrial Revolution, the expansion of markets on a world-wide scale, and the long period of peace prevailing under British world hegemony, commercial and other transactions increasingly took on a complex and long-range nature. The function of money became more and more that of a standard of deferred payments. Marshall pointed out that for this purpose, stability of value over time is the absolutely essential condition. However, the dynamics of economic patterns are such as to undermine such stable values.

Marshall noted that when people believe that general prices are going to rise, they rush in to purchase goods, increase production, borrowing surges, business is inflated, manufacturers increase production, borrowing surges, business is inflated, enterprises are managed recklessly and wastefully, and those working on borrowed capital pay back less real value than they borrowed, and enrich themselves at the expense of the community. This inflationary binge generates its own dynamics, feeding on itself, until the overextension is so great that the whole system collapses and causes a crash.

perform the function of standard of value for long-term obligations on the massive scale prevalent at his time. To preserve the integrity of the free enterprise system, and to create optimum conditions for the production and distribution of goods and services in line with demand and supply, a different standard of value would have to be devised. Such a standard should assure the essential stability of purchasing power of long-term obligations. Marshall recommended that an independent government agency be established to determine a representative purchasing power unit in terms of which long-term obligations would be calculated. He acknowledged that there would be practical problems involved in this procedure, but noted that even on a crude basis this approach would provide "a tenfold better standard of value than that afforded by the precious metals." As to public acceptance of this idea, he felt that while initially people might consider the notion of stable purchasing power units as unusual, they would accept them as soon as they recognized the substantial advantages accruing to everyone interested in a stable, fair, and sound economic system.

It is noteworthy that Marshall's observations were made approximately one hundred years ago. At that time, Great Britain and most other countries used precious metals as currency. Marshall specifically rejected gold and other precious metals as an adequate standard of value for long-term obligations. His conclusions apply even more forcefully to paper currencies, which have no intrinsic value whatsoever.

If Marshall was concerned about the scale of long-term transactions in his day, he would undoubtedly consider today's dimensions fantastic. Total long-term debt in the United States now exceeds $3 trillion, a sum that is far greater than world-wide production of goods and services throughout the nineteenth century.

In Marshall's time, inflationary periods were relatively short-lived and were invariably followed by deflationary ones. As a result, the long-term price trends in the nineteenth century showed considerable stability. Marshall's objective in recommending purchasing power units for long-term obligations was to prevent violent fluctuations in the business cycle that caused distortions and injustice by encouraging speculation on the value of money. In a period of chronic inflation, such as the United States has experienced since the New Deal days, Marshall's recommendations for tying long-term obligations to purchasing power units should be regarded as an essential procedure to prevent collapse of the financial structure.

It is apparent that both Adam Smith and Alfred Marshall have ideas of great relevance to our current inflationary predicament. In fact, had modern economists paid more attention to these classical thinkers we might have avoided many of our problems.

THE HOCUS-POCUS
OF FEDERAL FINANCE

A funny thing happens to the U.S. government debt on the way from the U.S. Treasury to the Federal Reserve. Common sense and plain logic would assume that a debt of the federal government is a debt, no matter which federal entity has possession of the certificate of indebtedness. But if you want to understand the esoterica of government finance as practiced today, you had better forget about common sense and logic and be prepared for some surprises. When the Federal Reserve acquires a government security, it issues a check drawn on itself and backed by nothing but its signature for the amount of the obligation. This check, which is newly created fiat money, is then deposited in a commercial bank. The latter is now enabled to use the government check as a new reserve asset, on the basis of which it can make loans and investments. As the funds move through the banking system, which operates on a fractional reserve basis, requiring only a small portion of deposits to be kept in the vaults, the overall effect is an estimated sevenfold increase in the availability of credit. Applying this procedure to the total Federal Reserve holdings of $96 billion of U.S. government securities and Federal Agency obligations as of July 21, 1976, banks could make loans and investments aggregating $672 billion.

Here is a more detailed explanation of the procedure involved in the Federal Reserve's transformation of federal debt obligations into new reserves of the banking system. Assume that the reserve ratio is 10 percent and that the Federal Reserve buys $100 worth of a government security. The sequence of events is as follows:

	Received by Bank	*Reserve Requirement*	*Loans or Investments*
Bank A	$100.00	$10.00	$90.00
Bank B	90.00	9.00	81.00
Bank C	81.00	8.10	72.90
Bank D	72.90	7.29	65.61
Bank E	65.61	6.56	59.05

This process continues until the full $100 received from the Federal Reserve has been transformed into incremental reserves and the banks have added $1,000 to their portfolios of loans and investments. Incidentally, it is not necessary for new banks to be involved at all levels. For example, if Bank E should be the same as Bank B, the dynamics would still be the same. The time that elapses between the Federal Reserve's initial purchase and the ultimate effect on loans and investments is relatively short, for the banks' earnings are directly affected by the speed with which they transform reserves into earning assets.

Actual reserve requirements currently in effect are as follows: 7 percent for banks with net demand deposits of $2 million or less; 9.5 percent for banks with net deposits of $2–10 million; 11.75 percent for banks with net deposits of $10–100 million; 12.75 percent for banks with net deposits of $100–400 million; and 16.25 percent for banks with net deposits of over $400 million. Thus, if all the Federal Reserve funds ended up in the smallest banks, the multiplier would be about 14 to 1. On the other extreme, if the biggest banks received all the incremental funds, the multiplier would be about 6 to 1. The 7-for-1 ratio assumed in this study is probably a conservative average estimate.

A clear distinction should be made between purchases of government securities by the Federal Reserve and by all other entities. The latter must, of course, pay for such securities with real funds that they earned or saved, rather than with fiat money. Furthermore, such purchases of government securities do not add to the reserve assets of the banking system; they merely shift funds from one source to another. Only the Federal Reserve can create new money by fiat and thus increase reserve assets of the banks.

Table I presents data on the federal government's deficits (surpluses), total indebtedness, Federal Reserve holdings of government securities, and the annual inflation rates for the period 1940 to 1975. Overall, the Federal Reserve increased its holdings of U.S. Treasury securities from $2.2 billion in 1940 to $87.9 billion in 1975. In addition, it has acquired almost $7 billion of Federal Agency obligations since 1971, which are not reflected in the table. For present purposes, these obligations have the same impact on the nation's financial affairs as U.S. Treasury holdings by the Federal Reserve. These data demonstrate the magnitude of the Federal Reserve's acquisition of government debt obligations. They have clearly become the major instrument of Federal Reserve policy.

The period covered in the table may be subdivided into three categories: (1) The World War II years, 1941–45, during which Federal Reserve holdings of government debt securities rose by about $22 billion; (2) The postwar period, 1946–57, characterized by basic stability in such holdings; (3) 1958 to the present, which shows a major upward spiral.

Table I

GOVERNMENT DEFICITS, DEBTS, AND INFLATION

Year	Deficits (Surplus)*	Total Debt*	Fed. Reserve Debt Holdings*	Inflation Rate %
1940	3.0	50.9	2.2	0.96
1941	5.0	64.3	2.3	5.00
1942	20.7	112.5	6.2	10.66
1943	54.9	170.1	11.5	6.15
1944	47.0	232.1	18.8	1.74
1945	47.5	278.7	24.3	2.28
1946	15.9	259.1	23.3	8.53
1947	(3.9)	256.9	22.6	14.36
1948	(12.0)	252.8	23.3	7.77
1949	(0.6)	257.1	18.9	(0.97)
1950	3.1	256.7	20.8	0.98
1951	6.1	259.4	23.8	7.90
1952	1.5	267.4	24.7	2.18
1953	6.5	275.2	25.9	0.75
1954	1.2	278.7	24.9	0.50
1955	3.0	280.8	24.8	(0.38)
1956	(4.1)	276.6	24.9	1.49
1957	(3.3)	274.9	24.2	3.56
1958	3.0	282.9	26.3	2.73
1959	12.9	290.8	26.6	0.81
1960	(0.3)	290.2	27.4	1.60
1961	3.4	296.2	28.9	1.01
1962	7.1	303.5	30.8	1.11
1963	4.7	309.3	33.6	1.21
1964	5.9	317.9	37.0	1.31
1965	1.6	320.9	40.8	1.72
1966	3.8	329.3	44.3	2.86
1967	8.7	344.7	49.1	2.88
1968	25.1	358.0	52.9	4.20
1969	(3.2)	368.2	57.2	5.37
1970	2.9	389.2	62.1	5.93
1971	23.0	424.1	70.2	4.30
1972	23.3	449.3	69.9	3.30
1973	14.3	469.9	78.5	6.23
1974	3.5	492.7	80.5	10.97
1975	43.6	576.6	87.9	9.14
1976 est.	66.5	643.1		
1977 est.	65.0	708.1		

*$billion.

Sources
Federal deficits (surpluses) were contained in the *Economic Report of the President*, January 1976.
Debt and Federal Reserve Holdings prior to 1946 were obtained from the *Economic Report of the President* for 1958; subsequent data came from the same source dated January 1976.
Inflation rates based on information supplied in *The Handbook of Basic Economic Statistics*, March 1976.
Estimated figures for 1976 and 1977 were cited in *U.S. News & World Report*, February 28, 1977.

26

During the World War II years of 1941–45, Federal Reserve holdings of U.S. Treasury securities jumped from $2.3 billion to $24.3 billion. At the time, reserve requirements of the Central Reserve City Banks were 24 percent. On this basis, the $22 billion net increase in Federal Reserve holdings of government obligations could be utilized by the banks to generate some $88 billion in new funds. This enabled the federal authorities to monetize about half of the deficits, aggregating to some $175 billion. This interval also witnessed some of the highest inflation rates in U.S. history. It should be noted that inflation rates did not reach their peak until 1947, when price controls were removed.

Between 1946 and 1957 Federal Reserve holdings of government debt remained unchanged at around $24 billion. Overall, this period was characterized by a considerable lessening of inflation rates. Two years stand out for indicating high correlations between Federal Reserve holdings of government securities and inflation rates. In 1949 the Federal Reserve reduced its government securities portfolio by over $4 billion, the only major reduction in the period 1940–75. It is not accidental that during 1949 the general price level declined by almost 1 percent, the only significant decline between 1940 and the present. Contrariwise, when the Federal Reserve increased its government debt holdings by $3 billion in 1951, the inflation rate jumped to 7.90 percent.

Since 1958 the Federal Reserve has added some $71 billion of government debt to its portfolio, including almost $7 billion Federal Agency obligations. On the basis of the estimated 7-for-1 leverage provided by the banking system, this could be transformed into $497 billion of new funds. In this interval, the government has added some $350 billion to its indebtedness. It is noteworthy that whereas during the World War II period the Federal Reserve supplied only half as much new money and credit as the aggregate federal deficits, in the most recent period it pumped approximately $1.50 into the money system for each $1 of federal deficits, or three times as much as during the World War II period. This indicates increased reliance on fiat money and credit as well as a lessened responsiveness of the financial system to such infusions. It is also apparent that the period 1958–75 saw an almost steady rise in inflation rates, reaching the double-digit level in 1974 for the first time since the World War II period. It takes no great genius to figure out that if trends in government finance and Federal Reserve holdings of federal obligations continue the pattern of recent years, double-digit inflation rates may well become the norm, rather than the exception.

The Federal Reserve can of course generate new funds in other ways, but nothing lends itself as readily to its fine-tuned intervention in the financial markets as its transactions in federal government obligations. The Federal Reserve is in the market daily to buy or sell such securities, depending on which way it wants the cat to jump. This procedure is used not only to control the funds available to the banking system, but also to influence interest rates. Ironically, the higher the government debt goes, the more leverage over the economy the Federal Reserve obtains. Contrariwise, if the federal debt were to disappear entirely, the Federal Reserve would be hard put to manipulate the money supply as readily. Government obligations now constitute some 80 percent of all the assets of the Federal Reserve. It is self-evident that the Federal Reserve has transformed these government debt holdings into the major fulcrum of the whole credit structure in this country. This is the contemporary equivalent for the practices by governments in the past of clipping coins or blending base metals into gold.

The transformation of federal debt obligations into a sevenfold generation of cash and credit has several ramifications of great significance: (1) It moves virtually all external financial restraints from the federal government; (2) it is the chief engine of inflation; (3) it saddles the government's creditors in particular, and savers in general, with the full burden of Washington's profligacies; and (4) it undermines the whole monetary system and jeopardizes free enterprise and democratic institutions.

The federal government is the only entity that can convert a debt into a new reserve asset. Similar legerdemain on the part of a private individual or corporation would be considered a combination of counterfeiting and other felonies. When people in the private sector want to borrow money, they have to meet all kinds of standards and obligations before the funds are made available. Furthermore, they have to expect constant surveillance by the creditors, who want to make sure that their funds are properly employed and safe. None of these restrictions apply to the federal government. It can shed all semblance of financial discipline, generating ever higher deficits and borrowing ever more, without the slightest concern that the funds might not be available on the next round of financing. The politicians and bureaucrats know only too well that there is no apparent limit to the Federal Reserve's capacity to meet all the government's financial requirements. Apparently, Washington believes in a basic division of labor for the economy as a whole: The private sector produces goods and services, while the federal establishment manufactures deficits and fiat money with which to finance them.

The Federal Reserve's monetary policies undoubtedly constitute the chief engine of inflation. All of the funds and credits generated by the conversion of government debt into new reserve assets of the banking system compete for the goods and services of the economy with the dollars that were earned and/or saved by the hard work of individuals and corporations in the private sector. The statistics clearly show the close correlation between Federal Reserve holdings of government securities and inflation rates. This should not be surprising when one considers the magnitude of the problem, for almost $700 billion of fiat money and credit are sufficient to undermine the viability of even the strongest economic system in the world. Government officials and politicians, with few exceptions, appear to be blind to these realities. Their apparent lack of insight enables them to blame others for their misdeeds. Time and again one hears voices in Washington clamoring for more controls over the private economy, as if the hard-working people were to be blamed for the unpleasant realities generated by the government's financial irresponsibilities. Moreover, insofar as politicians comment on the operations of the Federal Reserve, they invariably blame it for not doing enough to generate fiat money. This gives the impression that the Federal Reserve is doing its utmost to constrain politicians from wrecking the financial system. In actuality, in spite of its supposed independence the Federal Reserve has gone far in accommodating the politicians. In any case, let no one be duped by any double-talk out of Washington: The chronic inflation that has plagued this country for the past four decades is due solely to the government's financial manipulations.

Adam Smith, whose wisdom we require more than ever, noted in *Wealth of Nations* that whenever governments are heavily in debt, they use their control over currency to defraud their creditors. The transformation of government debt into cash and credit of the banking system via the Federal Reserve's creation of fiat money fully confirms the accuracy of the analysis made by the father of economic theory. The government's financial gains from inflation, and its creditors' losses, include: (1) Interest rates below inflation rates plus a normal return on capital; (2) tax receipts that are swelled by inflation's impact on graduated income tax rates; and (3) repayment of debts with depreciated currency.

In a truly free market environment, interest rates would long ago have risen to levels safeguarding creditors against loss of capital due to inflation. However, normal market mechanisms cannot work properly in an environment dominated by a massive violator of the rules of the game. When the banks are flooded with fiat funds generated by the Federal Reserve's debt monetizing operations, interest rates are of course depressed, as money to lend is readily available. This creates a topsy-turvy situation: The more fiat money is put in circulation, the less capable are interest rates of protecting creditors from loss of capital due to inflation. The deliberate undermining of normal interest rate functions is one of the most iniquitous aspects of the Federal Reserve's manipulations. The record clearly shows that throughout the period 1940–75, interest rates hardly ever were allowed to reflect fully inflation rates plus a normal return on capital. As a result, investors in government securities have lost tens of billions of dollars.

For example, in 1975 the government paid $31 billion interest on the $577 billion total indebtedness. Just to cover the inflation rate of 9.14 percent would have required $52.7 billion. Thus, investors in government securities lost over $21 billion on inflation in one year, not to mention any return on capital. These losses of investors, of course, represent gains to the government.

Investors in government securities are not the only victims of this interest rate distortion. Anyone with a savings account, a life insurance policy, a pension fund, or any other fixed-income asset whose rate of return is below the inflation rate suffers similar consequences. It should be noted that the interest rates on most savings instruments are also controlled by the federal government, either directly or indirectly. Clearly all the lenders and hardworking people who saved some money for a rainy day are penalized by the profligate spenders in government who have turned the rules of finance upside down for their own benefit.

The federal government also gains from inflation through higher income tax receipts. As inflation mounts year after year, the income of individuals and corporations increases in nominal terms, even though in a real sense—that is, in terms of purchasing power—there may be no increase at all. However, the tax collector benefits not merely in proportion to the increased income, but at ever higher rates in line with the higher income taxes on the ascending income tax brackets. Other gains to the Internal

Revenue Service include taxing the inflation factor in interest rates and increased income from corporations, whose depreciation and inventory accounting are penalized by chronic inflation. Chapter 5, "Benefits to the Tax Collector," describes these tax consequences of inflation in detail.

It is self-evident that when the government repays its debt it does so with depreciated dollars. For example, people who bought government bonds during the early 1940s and cash them in now will get less than twenty-five cents on the dollar in terms of purchasing power. How does that differ from bankruptcy? This is truly a tragic situation, for many of these bonds were purchased by patriotic citizens responding to their government's appeal to help finance the war effort. This same government has caused the inflation that resulted in the drastic loss of purchasing power of these bonds.

Apparently the federal managers of financial affairs have disregarded the effects of their policies on the monetary system. Money is supposed to fulfill three functions: (1) to act as a medium of exchange for immediately completed transactions; (2) to serve as a standard of value for all long-term transactions; and (3) to represent a store of value for savings and investments. The second and third functions are possible only if there is stability in the purchasing power of money over time The chronic inflation which has been our lot for the past four decades undermines and ultimately destroys these vital functions of money. For example, it would not be surprising if a recurrence of double-digit inflation could lead to the collapse of the long-term bond market. Similarly, when people find their savings eroded at excessive levels by inflation, they will sooner or later realize that it makes no sense to save anymore. Under extreme circumstances, even the function of money as a medium of exchange may be jeopardized. At the peak of the inflation that raged in Germany during the early 1920s, workers were paid twice a day to enable them to rush out to buy whatever they could before their earnings became worthless. It was not unusual to see the price of bread double in the course of a few hours.

The German example also shows the great risks to free enterprise and to democratic political institutions arising from chronic inflation. The latter wipes out the financial resources of all the prudent people who played by the rules, worked hard, and tried to save enough money to take care of their needs. These innocent victims of inflation also happen to be the mainstay of the free enterprise system and of the democratic political institutions. Once they realize that they have been defrauded by their own government, they join the ranks of the extremists and facilitate the emergence of dictatorships. Adam Smith noted that this is a common pattern discernible throughout history. The downfall of the Roman Republic because of its financial frauds against its own citizens is perhaps the earliest example.

Can anything be done at this late stage to stop and reverse this diabolical pattern in the United States today? The first step toward the restoration of sanity is to see the truth as it really is. We must recognize the fact that the chronic inflation that has plagued us for the past four decades is solely due to the government's irresponsible financial operations. Inflation is in effect a disguised form of governmental bankruptcy, whereby the government bails itself out of its financial obligations by penalizing its creditors and all savers. Far from getting something for nothing, as the politicians always try to make it appear has been the case, the American people have been hoodwinked by their own government into an increasingly intolerable situation.

Once people know the truth, appropriate policies to rectify the situation can be initiated. One basic principle should be that the federal government should not be the major beneficiary from the inflation which it causes, for such behavior may well violate the provision of the U.S. Constitution safeguarding peoples' property against deprivation without due process of law. Inflation-proofing of government securities and of income tax rates constitute appropriate steps along these lines. A basic reassessment of the Federal Reserve's functions and policies should be initiated as soon as possible. It is evident that our elected officials have transfered major powers over the purse strings to the Federal Reserve. The latter has in effect become a substitute for rational budget and tax procedures in accordance with the Constitution. Government bureaucrats and politicians should not have the option to be bailed out by inflation from their financial irresponsibilities. Further suggestions for solving the inflation problem are provided in Chapter 26, "Inflation Can Be Conquered."

Abraham Lincoln pointed out that you cannot fool all of the people all of the time. Once the voters of this country realize that the hocus-pocus of government finance is the real culprit in the inflation swindle, perhaps we will get the necessary support for policies that will restore sanity and integrity to our body politic.

THE GOVERNMENT DISTORTS THE RULES

Ever since the New Deal days of the 1930s, the U.S. government has placed itself outside the normal rules of finance. This fact is at the heart of the inflation problem. An examination of these rules and how they have been perverted will help clarify this issue.

Under normal circumstances, money disciplines economic behavior. Because money and economic resources are limited, expenditures have to be kept in line with income and savings. In a free market, this leads to the optimum allocation of resources on the basis of supply and demand. The New Dealers endeavored to overcome these limitations by pouring billions of dollars of fiat funds into the economy. In this fashion, they could escape the discipline of having to live within their means. However, this scheme has undermined the whole financial system and has created a condition of disguised national bankruptcy in the form of inflation. Moreover, the government has in effect penalized its creditors and all savers by forcing them to pay for its profligacies. Unfortunately, this behavior pattern was not limited to the Depression period, but has persisted for most of the past four decades.

Interest is the cost of money, which is normally determined by the demand for, and supply of, funds. There is no bias in favor of either borrowers or lenders. The New Deal brain trusters decided that interest rates should favor borrowers. The same fiat funds which undermine the purchasing power of money also push down interest rates, because they artificially increase the supply of money. The government, as the largest single borrower, thus gained major benefits at the expense of its creditors. As will be shown in Chapter 4, "Washington's Interest Rate Deception," this perversion of interest rates has persisted throughout the past four decades.

Normally, people work to earn money to take care of their needs. In addition, they will put some funds away in the form of savings for future requirements. Money is borrowed only under unusual circumstances, and care is taken to make sure that such loans can be repaid in full within a reasonable time. This ethic was completely turned around by the New Deal zealots. Their basic thrust was to spend money to achieve prosperity, even if that money had to be created by fiat. In addition to the government's deficit spending, they encouraged all others to live beyond their means, to spend now and pay later. Total national indebtedness in excess of $3 trillion by 1975 attests to their success in twisting the rules of finance to their ends.

This topsy-turvy approach to the rules of finance has many ramifications. It favors profligate spenders over savers. It makes a mockery of traditional values of prudence and thrift. It gives the government a virtually free hand to carry on its affairs without financial discipline. It undermines not only all orthodox financial realities, but also creates a general attitude of disobedience to established values and institutions. This new reality weakens society in basic ways and may jeopardize its very existence.

36

For rules to work, they are best applied universally, with impartiality. If a major participant in the financial sphere openly flouts the rules or twists them in his favor, he may cause the collapse of the whole system if he is not stopped in time. The rules of finance are too important to be left subject to the vagaries of self-serving politicians and bureaucrats. If we want to bring inflation to an end, we must insist that the government abide by the same rules of sound finance that everybody else does.

WASHINGTON'S INTEREST RATE DECEPTION

Interest is the cost of borrowing money. If there is any serious doubt about the loan being repaid in full by the borrower, the transaction is either not made at all or the interest rate is raised to compensate for this risk. Inflation is a process that reduces the purchasing power of money, which has the same effect as a lessened repayment of the loan. In a free economy, interest rates should fully reflect inflation rates to take care of this problem.

Ever since the New Deal days the federal government has pursued a deliberate policy of manipulating interest rates in favor of borrowers, notably itself. The following tables show the results of this endeavor in relation to investors in U.S. government securities. In order to place the problem in perspective, we have assumed that normal interest rates on U.S. treasury bills would have averaged 2 percent throughout this period. Similarly, normal interest rates on long-term bonds were assumed to be 3 percent. In both cases, inflation rates are calculated separately.

39

Table II

LOSSES BY INVESTORS IN 3-MONTH U.S. TREASURY BILLS

Year	Annual Inflation Rate (%)	Assumed Normal Yield (%)	Actual Yield (%)	Loss to Investors
1940	0.96	2.96	0.01	2.95
1941	5.00	7.00	0.10	6.90
1942	10.66	12.66	0.33	12.33
1943	6.15	8.15	0.37	7.78
1944	1.74	3.74	0.38	3.36
1945	2.28	4.28	0.38	3.90
1946	8.53	10.53	0.38	10.15
1947	14.36	16.36	0.59	16.77
1948	7.77	9.77	1.04	8.73
1949	(0.97)	1.03	1.10	(0.07)
1950	0.98	2.98	1.22	1.76
1951	7.90	9.90	1.55	8.35
1952	2.18	4.18	1.77	2.41
1953	0.75	2.75	1.93	0.82
1954	0.50	2.50	0.95	1.55
1955	(0.38)	1.62	1.75	(0.13)
1956	1.49	3.49	2.66	0.83
1957	3.56	5.56	3.27	2.29
1958	2.73	4.73	1.84	2.89
1959	0.81	2.81	3.41	(0.60)
1960	1.60	3.60	2.93	0.67
1961	1.01	3.01	2.38	0.63
1962	1.11	3.11	2.78	0.33
1963	1.21	3.21	3.16	0.05
1964	1.31	3.31	3.55	(0.24)
1965	1.72	3.72	3.95	(0.23)
1966	2.86	4.86	4.88	(0.02)
1967	2.88	4.88	4.32	0.56
1968	4.20	6.20	5.34	0.86
1969	5.37	7.37	6.68	0.69
1970	5.93	7.93	6.46	1.47
1971	4.30	6.30	4.35	1.95
1972	3.30	5.30	4.07	1.23
1973	6.23	8.23	7.04	1.19
1974	10.97	12.97	7.84	5.13
1975	9.14	11.14	5.80	5.34

Sources:
The Handbook of Basic Economic Statistics for inflation rates.
Economic Report of the President, February 1974, for U.S. Treasury Bill rates, 1940–73.
Federal Reserve Bulletins, for U.S. Treasury Bill rates since 1974.

Table III

LOSSES BY INVESTORS IN LONG-TERM U.S. GOVERNMENT BONDS

Year	Annual Inflation Rate (%)	Assumed Normal Yield (%)	Actual Yield (%)	Loss to Investors
1940	0.96	3.96	2.26	1.70
1941	5.00	8.00	2.05	5.95
1942	10.66	13.66	2.46	11.20
1943	6.15	9.15	2.47	6.68
1944	1.74	4.74	2.48	2.26
1945	2.28	5.28	2.37	2.91
1946	8.53	11.53	2.19	9.34
1947	14.36	17.36	2.25	15.11
1948	7.77	10.77	2.44	8.33
1949	(0.97)	2.03	2.31	(0.28)
1950	0.98	3.98	2.32	1.66
1951	7.90	10.90	2.57	8.43
1952	2.18	5.18	2.68	2.50
1953	0.75	3.75	2.94	0.81
1954	0.50	3.50	2.55	0.95
1955	(0.38)	2.62	2.84	(0.22)
1956	1.49	4.49	3.08	1.41
1957	3.56	6.56	3.47	3.09
1958	2.73	5.73	3.43	2.30
1959	0.81	3.81	4.07	(0.26)
1960	1.60	4.60	4.01	0.59
1961	1.01	4.01	3.90	0.11
1962	1.11	4.11	3.95	0.16
1963	1.21	4.21	4.00	0.21
1964	1.31	4.31	4.15	0.16
1965	1.72	4.72	4.21	0.51
1966	2.86	5.86	4.66	1.20
1967	2.88	5.88	4.85	1.03
1968	4.20	7.20	5.25	1.95
1969	5.37	8.37	6.10	2.27
1970	5.93	8.93	6.59	2.34
1971	4.30	7.30	5.74	1.56
1972	3.30	6.30	5.63	0.67
1973	6.23	9.23	6.30	2.93
1974	10.97	13.97	6.99	6.98
1975	9.14	12.14	6.98	5.16

Sources:
The Handbook of Basic Economic Statistics, for inflation rates.
Economic Report of the President, February 1974, for long-term government bond yields, 1940–73.
Federal Reserve Bulletin, for long-term bond yields since 1974.

Tables II and III are most revealing. According to the data, investors in U.S. treasury bills lost money in all but six years during the period 1940–75. To convert these data into dollars and cents, let us assume that an investor purchased a treasury bill in 1940 for $1,000 and kept on turning over the proceeds as they matured throughout the next thirty-six years. He should have collected $720 in interest ($20 a year for thirty-six years) plus $1,401.40 to cover the inflation rates, for a total of $2,121.40. Instead, he collected only $1,005.60, leaving him with a loss of $1,115.80. It is interesting to note that investors would have been in a better position had they been merely guaranteed against inflation, without any interest whatsoever.

The table on long-term bonds reveals similar results. Investors lost money in all but three years during the period 1940–75. Converting these data into dollars and cents, let us assume that an investor purchased a long-term bond in 1940 for $1,000 and turned it over for a new long-term bond every year thereafter, to take advantage of the higher yields that became available as time went on. (If he had kept the funds in the bond he purchased in 1940 his losses would be even more staggering.) He should have collected $1,080 interest ($30 a year for thirty-six years) plus $1,401.40 to cover the cumulative inflation, for a total of $2,481.40. Instead, he collected only $1,365.40, leaving him with a loss of $1,116. Again, investors would have improved their lot if they had loaned the government their money free of any interest, just to obtain protection from inflation. This reality is magnified by the fact that most private investors have to pay substantial taxes on the interest income they receive, adding insult to injury.

To demonstrate the losses to investors in just one year, let us take the data applicable for 1975. If an investor purchased a treasury bill for $1,000, his actual yield for the year was $58. The assumed normal yield would have been $111.40. Thus, he sustained a loss of $53.40. Even without return on capital, he lost $33.40 on inflation alone. Similarly, on a long-term bond his yield for the year would have averaged $69.80 per bond. The assumed normal yield would have been $121.40; he therefore lost $51.60 per bond. Assuming no return on capital, he lost $21.60 on inflation alone.

Altogether, in 1975 the federal government paid $31 billion interest on the $577 billion total indebtedness. Just to cover the inflation rate of 9.14 percent would have required $52.7 billion. Thus, investors in government securities lost over $21 billion on inflation in one year, not to mention any return on capital.

It should be noted that these losses of investors in government securities are direct gains for the U.S. government. The decline in purchasing power of money means that the government can pay back in cheaper dollars whatever it borrows. Moreover, far from being an innocent party in this process, the government plays the key role in generating inflation as an integral part of its interest rate manipulations.

How does the government achieve these results? The manipulation of interest rates is carried out in part by statutory limits on what competitive savings institutions can pay to their depositors, and in part by open market operations of the Federal Reserve. The latter controls money, credit, and interest rates by using fiat money to convert government debt issues into new reserve assets of the banking system. Since 1940 the Federal Reserve has acquired close to $100 billion of such government obligations, paying for them with checks drawn on itself. As the checks pass through the banking system, which operates on a fractional reserve basis, they are converted into an estimated $700 billion of money and credit. Interest rates are of course pushed down by this massive infusion of fiat funds. Under these conditions, interest rates cannot fulfill their function of protecting creditors from ruinous losses. It demonstrates the reality that normal financial mechanisms cannot work properly in an environment dominated by a government agency that does not abide by the rules of sound finance. As a result, it is self-evident that a truly free market in interest rates has not existed since the 1930s.

In effect, the government deprives investors in its securities of a substantial portion of their property by deliberately following policies that reduce interest rates below the levels necessary to protect investors from this confiscatory pattern. All of this manipulation is done in the name of "stabilizing the economy" or even "fighting inflation." I suppose if one asked a fox what he is doing in the chicken coop, he would answer, "I am here to keep order." When the game is over, the chicken are gone; so will the nation's wealth be gone if we do not stop the prevailing practices in relation to interest rates.

To be fair to the government, there is no lack of voices from political pressure groups demanding the continuation and even acceleration of the process of undermining the currency and manipulating interest rates in favor of borrowers. What all these pressure groups overlook is the fact that this systematic manipulation of interest rates in favor of profligate spenders at the expense of savers is the source of most of the economic ills currently plaguing us. Inflation is without doubt the direct outgrowth of this policy. The general breakdown in financial discipline, the predominant pattern of living beyond one's means, the emergence of cartels in key areas, and the resulting distortions of economic processes are all manifestations of this pattern. Interest rate manipulations and inflation, which had originally been proposed as deliberate policies to pull the country out of economic difficulties, have now become major causes of the very problems they were designed to cure. Nothing could more vividly demonstrate the propensity of governments to act in counterproductive ways.

Those in the government will undoubtedly claim that they have no intention of deliberately defrauding investors in its securities. The sincerity of this assertion can be readily tested by the willingness of the members of the government to institute corrective procedures. In determining the appropriate yield on U.S. treasury bills, for instance, the government should either use the preceding three months' average rate of inflation as the basis, or else it should add the actual rate of inflation during the life of the bills to the pay-out at maturity. As the record shows, *any* interest rate above inflation rates would be a gain for investors compared with present procedures. Similarly, on long-term bonds the inflation rates during the life of the bonds should be calculated into the return to investors. A more detailed analysis of this procedure is presented in Chapter 27, "Inflation-Proof Government Securities."

Rationalizations about grand strategy for national policy have tended to obscure the relationship between inflation and interest rates, to the detriment of investors. If the U.S. government were to engage in a deliberate swindle it could not have done a better job of depriving its creditors of their property. It is imperative that all possible steps be taken to put an end to procedures that are economically unsound, morally reprehensible, and constitutionally unjustifiable.

5

BENEFITS
TO THE TAX COLLECTOR

Inflation provides billions of dollars of windfall gains to the tax collector. Escalating income tax rates take a disproportionate share of any increase in income that happens because of inflation. The inflation adjustment of interest rates is fully taxed even though it does not represent income at all. Business tax rates are increased by unrealistic depreciation policies and inventory calculations that do not reflect inflationary realities.

The tax distortions of inflation may be highlighted by assuming five years of double-digit price increases. If incomes kept pace, this would put almost everybody into the highest income tax brackets, even though incomes in real terms (purchasing power) had not increased at all. Because of the higher tax rates, everyone's standard of living would decline.

Normal interest rates represent income on capital. As such, the latter is subject to income tax. In the chronic inflationary environment that has prevailed over the past several decades, interest rates have gradually moved up to reflect in part these losses of capital. This inflation protection is obviously not income at all, but an attempt to safeguard capital from erosion. For example, if an investor purchases a government bond with a yield of 8 percent, it is reasonable to assume that 5 percent of this yield represents inflation insurance over the life of the bond. However, to the tax collector this reality is irrelevant; he will collect taxes on the full 8 percent. This is a vivid illustration of the fact that savers cannot protect themselves against the insidious forces of inflation, unless the government returns to fair dealings.

The tax bills of businesses are adversely affected by inflation in many ways. For example, in line with the general rise in prices, inventories held by corporations will rise in monetary terms and cause paper profits, particularly on those items in the inventory bought earlier at lower prices. These profits are of course taxed. In actual fact, however, the business enterprises will find themselves on a treadmill, for in a period of chronic inflation prices continue rising and the so-called paper profits become illusory, while the tax bills are very real. One procedure for minimizing this pattern is to put inventories on a LIFO (last in, first out) method of accounting, where the inventory purchased last is sold first.

Depreciation rates become increasingly obsolete in a chronic inflationary environment. The costs of constructing new factories, refineries, mines, and other capital assets have skyrocketed far in excess of depreciation schedules. Corporations are therefore forced to find outside sources of capital, because the internal cash generation is insufficient. Thus, the tax collector helps to undermine the financial viability of business firms.

These examples show that inflation has severe negative effects on taxpayers, both individual and corporate, while being of benefit only to the tax collector. Everything possible should be done to rectify this situation, particularly in view of the fact that the government has the responsibility for causing the inflation. There are indications of a more realistic attitude toward this problem by at least some government officials. Former Senator James L. Buckley introduced Bill S. 987, which provides for cost-of-living adjustments of income tax rates and depreciation deductions. Similarly, former Secretary of the Treasury William E. Simon has expressed himself in favor of indexing a portion of the income tax system against inflation (*U.S. News & World Report*, March 10, 1975). It is to be hoped that individuals and businesses will make every possible effort to support and expand these policies toward a saner, fairer tax system.

The tax structure should be fundamentally overhauled to reflect inflationary realities. Pious assertions about bringing inflation under control are no substitute for realistic measures to deal with the situation that actually exists. This is particularly true in view of the fact that the proponents of talk rather than action are invariably the politicians and bureaucrats who are responsible for causing inflation and who want to extract all possible benefits to themselves from it.

UNCLE SAM'S INFLATED CREDIT RATING

Between 1975 and 1977 the U.S. government will borrow more than $150 billion to cover new deficits incurred. This averages out to about $1 billion of new funds a week. In addition, the government will have to refinance an estimated average of $5 billion of its outstanding debt every week. Total indebtedness will exceed $700 billion in 1977. In view of the enormity of these operations, it seems remarkable how silent the financial community remains as to the credit-worthiness of the government. It appears as if everyone assumes that government obligations are worthy of the highest credit rating, no matter what financial mess the government gets itself into.

Under normal conditions, here are some of the questions that are raised by prospective lenders when they are approached about loans: (1) What is the magnitude of the total debt outstanding? (2) Are there any contingent liabilities? (3) What are the maturity schedules of the debt? (4) What are the interest charges? (5) What are the financial resources of the borrower? (6) Is there evidence that the borrower is chronically living beyond his means? If the answer to any of these questions is unsatisfactory, the credit rating of the borrower is lowered. A combination of several negative findings could make it difficult if not impossible for the borrower to obtain new loans.

There has never been a peacetime period when deficits approached the current levels. The only comparable period was that of the World War II years, 1941–45, when deficits totaled $170 billion.

Even these data do not tell the full story, for the U.S. government has also acquired enormous contingent liabilities. Some of the latter are almost indistinguishable from outright government obligations, such as the debts of federal agencies, which aggregate over $100 billion and are growing rapidly. In addition, the government has guaranteed insurance, loans, pensions, and international obligations in excess of $2 trillion, or three times the national debt (*U.S. News & World Report*, October 4, 1976). Under adverse circumstances, substantial amounts of these contingent liabilities could become real obligations.

The maturity schedules of the government debt should dismay any lender. The average life of the government's debt is down to 2½ years. At current levels of indebtedness, this means that approximately $5 billion of outstanding debt has to be refinanced every week, in addition to the $1 billion of new debt mentioned earlier.

The financial resources of the government are the taxes and other incomes it collects, plus the assets it holds. The taxes are close to the maximum levels one can reasonably expect. The same is true of most other sources of income. Asset management could probably be improved, but it would not represent a major source of additional revenue. The prospects for bringing deficits under control and repaying debts are not promising, particularly in view of the fact that the government has the propensity to take on ever more tasks and obligations.

The evidence that the government is chronically living beyond its means is overwhelming. Since 1940, the government has incurred deficits in twenty-eight years and surpluses in eight. The deficits aggregated over $450 billion and the surpluses $35 billion. During the last fifteen years deficits were shown annually with the sole exception of 1969. There is no early end in sight for this red ink.

The only positive feature in the government's financial status is the interest charges. The government pays the lowest interest rates of any borrower. However, this positive indicator does not stand up under critical inquiry. The low interest rates result from the government's financial manipulations, not from wise management.

On the basis of this assessment, the realistic lender might well conclude that the government is not creditworthy and that new loans should be refused. But no such conclusion is likely to stand in the way of government financing. The government has placed itself outside the normal rules of finance by using its control over the currency to take care of its needs without subjecting itself to outside discipline.

As has been shown in Chapter 2, "The Hocus-Pocus of Federal Finance," during the past four decades the U.S. government via the banks has poured an estimated $700 billion of fiat funds into the economy. This procedure has assured the government all the funds it needs for its operations. The infusion of fiat money has also pushed down interest rates to the government's advantage. In effect, the U.S. government's high credit rating is based on its financial manipulations, not on any sound financial stature.

The free enterprise system has great resiliency, as its record in this country has shown over the past two hundred years. However, it cannot survive the systematic, uninterrupted undermining of all normal rules of financial discipline by government. The government acts like a partner who not only takes a big share of the profits openly in the form of taxes, but also steals part of everyone else's portion secretly through inflation. In trying to get something for nothing, Uncle Sam is making everyone else foot the bill for his extravagances. The danger is very real that this procedure, on an unprecedented scale, will destroy our free economic and political institutions.

On the basis of normal credit rating criteria, the U.S. government is virtually insolvent. Credit ratings are designed to make all parties aware of the realities that must govern the relationship of borrowers and lenders. Systematic subversion of normal credit procedures by the biggest single borrower has dangerous implications for the whole financial system. It is therefore imperative that steps be taken to restore discipline and soundness to the government's financial operations before it is too late.

WHO IS RESPONSIBLE?

The financial policies of the federal government, operating outside the framework of the market system, are responsible for the chronic inflation now afflicting the United States. This effect is due to the fact that those involved in policy making apparently lack the proper perspective on the ramifications and long-term consequences of their decisions.

The Depression of the 1930s was the source of the policies that have led to inflation. That was an emergency situation, politically conducive to precipitous actions. If the programs started in the Depression had been confined to a short period of time, much of the ensuing problems could have been avoided. However, the bureaucracies that were set up to administer the various programs developed a life of their own and found ways of perpetuating and increasing their activities and power. Special-interest groups endeavored to influence legislation in their favor. Politicians sought to profit from the situation by sponsoring legislation of immediate appeal to many constituents. Almost everyone involved in the practical game of politics found it advantageous to play along with these policies, whose overall effect was to enlarge the powers of government, increase the number of its personnel, exempt it from financial discipline, and weaken the free enterprise economy.

The intellectual rationale for this New Deal program was provided by the writings of the British economist John Maynard Keynes. In his works he disregarded the warnings of classical economists against government intervention in the economy, with its bureaucratization of decision making and its propensity for replacing one existing evil with several new ones. Inflation is the natural outgrowth of all of these endeavors.

The U.S. government is structured in such a way as to provide a system of checks and balances to prevent possible abuses. Unfortunately, this structure did not prevent the trend toward the government's financial irresponsibility and its inevitable outgrowth, chronic inflation. An examination of the various factors involved in financial affairs will demonstrate this fact.

Most of the presidents since the 1930s have been actively endeavoring to increase the role of the federal government in the economic sphere. The discipline of the marketplace was an obstacle to their political ambitions. Therefore, they sought to weaken or remove these restrictions on their freedom of action. President Eisenhower was the only one who consistently moved against this trend. It is interesting to note that the rate of deficit spending and of inflation decreased significantly during his years in office. His contribution to financial responsibility by the federal government has not been sufficiently recognized. Had his successors continued along the lines he started, we would not find ourselves in the present predicament.

Congress has generally favored policies that increased the government's role in the economy. Spending public money has great appeal to most politicians, as it gives them influence and power. If all these programs had to be paid for on a current basis, the constituents would soon voice their displeasure about the mounting tax burden. The ideal situation for politicians is to spend ever more and tax ever less. This formula for political success happens to be the specific prescription for financial irresponsibility, including deficit spending, ever larger debts, and chronic inflation.

The agencies most directly involved with financial affairs are the U.S. Treasury and the Federal Reserve. Together, they have evolved procedures that are at the heart of the inflation problem. They developed the technique of using fiat funds to convert part of the government debt into new reserve assets of the banking system. This leveraged infusion of fiat funds into the economy serves two government objectives: (1) to make sure that its financing operations run smoothly; and (2) to keep interest rates low. Looked at objectively this procedure has more in common with legalized counterfeiting than with normal financial operations. It is a practice unworthy of regular usage by a democratic government. Unfortunately, it seems to have become a permanent fixture.

While everyone in government will undoubtedly try to pass the buck as to who causes inflation, the Federal Reserve's case is the weakest. The latter is supposed to be the guardian of sound money; instead, it has cooperated with the Treasury in developing techniques that undermine the purchasing power of the dollar. The Federal Reserve all along should have taken the position that chronic federal deficits made normal, noninflationary financing procedures almost impossible. At the least, it should have pioneered efforts to protect innocent parties, notably savers and the government's creditors, against losses due to inflation. Perhaps we are expecting too much, but the Federal Reserve ideally should be the financial conscience of the government.

It is clear from this survey that the agencies of government cannot be relied upon to bring inflation under control voluntarily. It is therefore imperative that an informed citizenry bring pressure to bear to reverse this situation. Politicians must be confronted with the fact that it is good politics to avoid financial irresponsibility by the one means they understand best—namely, the ballot box. The agencies of the government must be placed under appropriate guidelines to make sure that the property rights of creditors and savers are respected in line with constitutional guarantees.

It is to be hoped that henceforth all members of the federal establishment will place top priority on financial responsibility and the avoidance of inflationary procedures. This must become everybody's first order of business. The stake of the government in this matter cannot be overemphasized, for the battle against inflation may well involve the very survival of our political system.

THE LEGACY
OF KEYNES AND ROOSEVELT

John Maynard Keynes, the British economist, played a key role in providing the intellectual framework for the New Deal. His book *The General Theory of Employment, Interest, and Money* (MacMillan & Co. Ltd., London, 1936) repudiated laissez-faire classical economic theory and urged the government to determine economic events. His theories fell on receptive ears at the White House, whose occupant recognized the political values of such an approach.

In essence, the work of Keynes cited above was a prescription for changing the rules of economics and finance. Instead of relying on the "unseen hand of the marketplace" to determine the allocation of resources, interest rates, and money flows, he recommended that the government actively manipulate events in the economic sphere. During a depression, the government should generate deficits to stimulate the economy to provide jobs and income. Borrowing should be encouraged by monetary measures that would lower interest rates.

Franklin Delano Roosevelt had been elected to the presidency of the United States in 1932—the peak of the Depression—to move the country out of its predicament. As a master politician, he knew that an activist stance was just what the country wanted. This fact alone would have made him receptive to the ideas of Keynes. In addition, his own life-style may have predisposed him to such an orientation. As the offspring of a wealthy family, he may well have lived under the illusion that wealth is created by spending money. The fact that his forefathers had had to earn and save the money so that he could live without want may have escaped him. In any case, Keynes was enthroned as the new economic messiah in Washington.

Ironically, the Keynesian prescription was largely counterproductive during the Depression period. Government manipulations of the economy, deficit spending, and bureaucratic controls did not restore confidence. The business community distrusted it. Economic activity stayed at a low ebb throughout the 1930s. The greatest stimulant to economic recovery was not Keynesian economics but the outbreak of World War II. The latter quickly brought about full employment of resources and the end of all the other Depression symptoms. In this context, which was the antithesis of the framework for which Keynes had recommended his program, the politicians and bureaucrats in Washington engaged in massive deficit spending, fiat money creation, and interest rate manipulations designed to encourage borrowing. Such actions were a vivid demonstration of the government's propensity to do the wrong thing at the wrong time. Even Plato discovered some 2,500 years ago that the task of governing is not conducive to the triumph of wisdom or even common sense. Adam Smith warned repeatedly that governments tend to be stupid, profligate, and self-serving. Keynes, who was well grounded in classical thinking, should have known better than to entrust his ideas to government bureaucrats.

If one examines the earlier writings of Keynes, one finds that he was not unaware of inflationary dangers. In an essay entitled "Inflation," which Keynes wrote in 1919, he noted: "Lenin was certainly right, there is no subtler, no surer means of overturning the existing basis of society than to debauch the currency. The process engages all the hidden forces of economic law on the side of destruction and does it in a manner which not one man in a million is able to diagnose." *Essays in Persuasion*, Harcourt, Brace & Co., New York, 1932.

Unfortunately, Keynes seems to have disregarded these insights when he recommended policies in the 1930s that played right into the hands of the currency debauchers.

The historical record indicates that Roosevelt and Keynes played major roles in laying the foundation for government policies that have fostered chronic inflation during the past four decades. Their legacy should be carefully examined to eliminate obsolete and counterproductive ideas and practices.

9

THE CLAY FEET
OF THE FEDERAL RESERVE

The central role of the Federal Reserve in causing inflation results from several factors. The specter of the Great Depression of the 1930s left a permanent imprint on Federal Reserve policies, with counterproductive consequences. In fulfilling a variety of functions, the Federal Reserve has generally placed the lowest priority on maintaining the stability of the dollar's purchasing power. The separation of ethics from economics has facilitated policies that defraud the government's creditors and taxpayers, as well as savers. Confusion about the nature of money may also have contributed to the predicament.

During the Great Depression of the 1930s, the government initiated policies designed to increase the money supply and to lower interest rates. Whatever the merits of such policies for fighting depressions, they are clearly unsound if they become permanent fixtures regardless of economic and financial circumstances. Keynes had obviously underestimated the propensity of politicians and bureaucrats to stick with policies once they are operational and familiar. Keeping the economy flush with money and preventing interest rates from reflecting financial realities have become cornerstones of Federal Reserve policy since the 1930s, with obvious inflationary implications.

The Federal Reserve's Open Market Committee was created during the New Deal. It implements policies of the Board of Governors of the Federal Reserve on a day-by-day basis. One of its chief activities is the purchase and sale of government securities to influence the money supply and interest rates. As the government's indebtedness grew during the Depression and the World War II years, the Open Market Committee perfected the technique of debt monetizing by converting government securities acquired with fiat money into new reserve assets of the banking system. As was shown in Chapter 2, "The Hocus-Pocus of Federal Finance," this procedure is at the heart of the inflation process.

The bureaucrats running the Open Market Committee have increasingly relied on this tool of leveraged fiat money because it seems to work so effectively in accomplishing their purposes. Naturally it works—it has all of the advantages of counterfeiting and none of its disadvantages. In fact, if done on a sufficient scale over a period of time this procedure will undermine the whole monetary system. We have already advanced far along these lines.

The Federal Reserve has several tasks in relation to the domestic economy: (1) to supervise its member banks; (2) to facilitate the federal government's debt financing; (3) to provide an elastic monetary structure for the economy; and (4) to safeguard the stable purchasing power of money.

In actual practice, the results clearly show that safeguarding the stable purchasing power of the dollar has been overshadowed by the other tasks. The U.S Treasury and other government borrowers are of course eager to obtain all the funds they need at the lowest possible interest costs. In his study entitled *The Federal Reserve System*, (American Institute of Banking, 1972) Professor

Benjamin H. Beckhart states the case succinctly: "The [Federal] Reserve system frequently fell under Treasury influence and control. This was true during and after World Wars I and II, through the Great Depression, and much of the 1960's. . . . Secretaries of the Treasury are usually interested in the maintenance of low interest rates and a favorable climate for the flotation of federal obligations, even at the risk of price inflation."

The concept of an "elastic" monetary structure was designed to create more stable financial conditions and to prevent excessive swings in the monetary area. It is noteworthy that the term "elastic" is defined in the dictionary as "capable of returning to its original shape, after being stretched." This has been distorted by the bureaucrats into a condition of permanent and even larger stretch. Even the most elastic entity will break at some point if it is stretched too far. The record shows that the so-called elasticity of the monetary structure has been a one-way street during the past several decades, with all stretch and no return to the rest condition. This is another way of describing the inflationary pattern.

Perhaps the biggest single difference between contemporary financial-economic theory and that of the classical school relates to the ethical dimension. Classical economic theory is inconceivable without ethics; in fact, to the classical thinkers economics was an applied form of ethics. In contrast, twentieth-century economists generally consider economics a science that is quite separate from value judgments. This approach facilitates financial policies that from an ethical standpoint are highly questionable if not outright fraudulent. Most modern economists seem to be confused about the nature of inflation. Many even take the position that a "moderate amount" of inflation is beneficial to the economy. Adam Smith avoided such confusion. He stated that the government's manipulation of currency is invariably an evil practice designed to defraud its creditors. The Federal Reserve has followed procedures which have placed low priority on the rights of the government's creditors, taxpayers, and savers. This moral blindness has undoubtedly contributed to the inflation predicament.

Money is one of the oldest social inventions, and yet it has remained one of the most mysterious. Everyone has some notions about money, but very few persons, if any, seem to understand its many ramifications. The confusion is compounded when one tries to understand an entity like the Federal Reserve. There is probably no government agency with more powers, and fewer limitations, than those enjoyed by the Federal Reserve. The very confusion about money plays into the hands of this entity. In actual fact, the people who run the Federal Reserve are not all-wise deities. The record shows that they, too, have failed to understand the nature of money. Inflation is the loud and clear signal of their failure. Their ingenious scheme for using fiat money to convert government debt into new reserve assets of the banking system has backfired and revealed their clay feet.

Near the conclusion of his study of the Federal Reserve, Professor Beckhart expresses concern about the future of our financial system: "Throughout history governments have been very adept at adopting policies, often with declared motives of highest altruism, which have debased and depreciated currencies and which finally rendered them worthless." It is salutary for the American people to know these realities and to avoid placing reliance on false gods.

CHRONIC INFLATION
IS NOT ROOTED
IN AMERICAN HISTORY

If George Washington had visited the United States in 1940, he would have found that the value of the money he saved in 1790 had remained intact throughout the first hundred and fifty years of the Republic's existence. A return visit in 1976 would be most disheartening, for he would learn that his money had lost close to three-quarters of its purchasing power during the past thirty-six years. A perspective on the difference between these historical epochs should help shed light on the causes of inflation.

Keeping the purchasing power of the dollar intact was the primary financial objective of governments throughout our formative years. There were inflationary episodes connected with the War of 1812, the Civil War, and World War I. In each case, however, the inflationary upsurge was followed by a downswing in general price levels that erased the preceding upswing. The government made no effort to prevent these adjustments. It kept faith with its creditors and repaid its debts. It also lived within

67

its means. For example, between 1789 and 1849, government receipts totaled $1,160 million, outlays $1,090 million, leaving a surplus of $70 million (*The Budget of the U.S. Government, Fiscal Year 1977*, Government Printing Office, 1976). It is revealing to note that currently our government spends in one day what it took its predecessors sixty years to spend in the early part of our history.

Chronic inflation is without doubt the outgrowth of financial policies initiated during the New Deal. These included deliberate manipulations of the money supply to favor borrowers, notably the government itself. By pouring vast amounts of fiat funds into the banking system, the Federal Reserve pushed interest rates down and inflation rates up. This has been government policy for about four decades. It fully accounts for the inflation pattern that has plagued this country ever since.

Those who argue that we are living in more complex times than our forefathers have not properly read or understood history. The United States has always faced difficult and complex problems. What was different about our forefathers is that they endeavored to solve these problems in a manner that was in accord with constitutional provisions, classical economic principles, and basic honesty. The New Deal flouted all of these, with the results now apparent. It was not the complex conditions that caused inflation, but the manner in which the New Deal responded to these conditions.

Another fallacious argument concerns the relationship between chronic inflation and the free enterprise system. Critics of the latter try to blame inflation on advanced forms of capitalism. This has no foundation in reality. In a truly free market, which is at the heart of free enterprise, inflation would be quickly halted by interest rates that fully reflect inflation rates plus a normal return on investment. If no one benefits from inflation, there will be no inflation. Inflation can flourish only if the government deliberately manipulates interest rates in favor of borrowers, as ours has done during the past four decades. The inflation plaguing this country is the invention and legacy of the New Deal and its followers of both political parties in government.

It is imperative that the American people and their government awaken to these realities. It is totally inaccurate to justify our present inflationary predicament on the basis of American history or the supposed weaknesses of free enterprise. Our inflation was made by the New Deal, which initiated wrong policies in relation to money. There is no excuse for any government in power now blindly to follow monetary procedures that have no basis in American history and that are clearly counterproductive.

DEFINING THE SWINDLE

The dictionary defines the verb *swindle* as (1) to cheat out of money or other assets; (2) to obtain by fraud or deceit. The word is derived from the German word *Schwindler*, a giddy-minded, irresponsible person who defrauds others (*Random House College Dictionary*).

From a practical standpoint, a distinction should be made between a swindle that is deliberate and one that is an accidental occurrence. Similarly, a chronic pattern of swindling is obviously more iniquitous than an occasional transgression. People also tend to differentiate between swindles on the basis of who benefits from them. The most famous example is provided by the legendary twelfth-century English outlaw Robin Hood, who robbed the rich and gave to the poor. While his actions were clearly illegal, many people were inclined to forgive him because of his supposedly kind motivations.

Is inflation a swindle in terms of the dictionary definition cited above? There is no doubt that savers, taxpayers, and investors in government securities are being cheated out of money or other assets by inflation. Moreover, the evidence is overwhelming that the Federal Reserve, an agency of the government, causes inflation by converting federal debt securities acquired with fiat money into new reserve assets of the banking system, a deceptive if not outright fraudulent procedure in itself.

Is this swindle deliberate? The most generous interpretation is to give the government the benefit of the doubt and answer in the negative, with qualifications. There is no evidence of a deliberate conspiracy to cause inflation and/or to defraud the creditors of the U.S. government. However, the government has followed policies that have made inflation inevitable and that have given the lowest priority to maintaining a stable currency. At the least, those who run the government are guilty of the sin of omission, of neglecting their responsibilities to the government's creditors, taxpayers, and to the savers of this country.

The chronic nature of inflation over the past several decades greatly strengthens the case against the government. Since 1940, inflation occurred in all but two years. Investors in government securities lost money in all but three years. One would imagine that if the government were a truly innocent party, its leaders would be receptive to reasonable suggestions for rectifying the situation. For example, I have tried since 1970 to induce the government to issue inflation-proof bonds to protect its creditors from the inroads of inflation. U.S. Treasury officials have repeatedly rejected such proposals.

It has been suggested by some that inflation has the desirable feature of facilitating the transfer of wealth from the rich to the poor, a modern variation on the Robin Hood theme. This argument does not stand up under critical examination. First of all, inflation is harmful to all segments of society. While it undoubtedly hurts the rich, it is most devastating to the middle classes, including the vast majority of workers, small businessmen, pensioners, and farmers. These are the people whose incomes and savings are being eroded relentlessly by inflation. There is little evidence to support the notion that the poor are being helped by inflation. They may have a few more dollars with which to pay their bills, but their expenses have risen at least proportionately. Finally, the Robin Hood thesis falls flat on its face because from all indications the main beneficiary of the inflation swindle is the very perpetrator of that crime—namely, the federal government itself. Robin Hood committed crimes for the benefit of others; the U.S. government is not that altruistic.

Most contemporary economists try to avoid value judgments about government behavior. This policy seems to me to be a combination of intellectual blindness and moral cowardice. In their endeavor to be "objective" and "scientific," these economists have failed to recognize the ethical realities inherent in all human relations. Questions of right and wrong must be faced by governments as well as by individuals. Economics without ethics is a worthless discipline. In fact, many economists have assisted the government in developing the techniques and procedures that are at the heart of the inflationary process. This is in sharp contrast to the position of Adam Smith, who was fully aware of the close relationship between ethics and economics; he was professor of moral philosophy at Glasgow University while he worked on his *Wealth of Nations*. He did not hesitate to condemn governments for their immoral acts. In fact, he considered governments in general to be inclined to do evil, ready to defraud their creditors at any opportunity. The realities of history strongly support his position.

Our founding fathers also were aware of the tendency of governments to become tyrannical and immoral. Therefore, they put safeguards into the Constitution to protect the people from such governmental behavior. It should be noted that inflation is a form of taxation without representation that dwarfs anything the British ever did to their colonies in the eighteenth century.

Defining the Swindle

The time has come to expose inflation for what it really is—namely, a swindle perpetrated by the government in the furtherance of its own financial irresponsibilities at the expense of its creditors and the vast majority of the people. There is no excuse for this swindle on moral, constitutional, or practical grounds. There are ways of running the financial affairs of the United States without inflation; these should be implemented as soon as possible.

INFLATION
IGNORES CONSTITUTIONAL
SAFEGUARDS

Article I, Section 8 of the U.S. Constitution provides that the Congress shall have power to coin money and regulate the value thereof. This is immediately followed by the provision for "the punishment of counterfeiting the securities and current coin of the United States." It is apparent that the bureaucrats running the Federal Reserve have interpreted these constitutional stipulations to mean that they have unlimited powers to manipulate the money supply, and that the counterfeiting prohibition does not apply to them. This position is rather dubious, particularly when viewed in the context that the procedures employed have had many harmful effects on the fundamental rights of citizens and on the responsible functioning of their elected government.

The Fifth Amendment of the U.S. Constitution provides that "No person shall be . . . deprived of life, liberty, or property, without due process of law." Inflation deprives people of their property on a massive scale. In

1975 alone, investors in U.S. government securities lost over $21 billion in interest payments that did not reflect inflation rates. Other billions of dollars were lost by taxpayers because of inflation's impact on the graduated income tax system. Savers have found their property eroded on a massive scale by inflation. Moreover, the federal government has been the chief beneficiary of inflation. This process has been going on almost uninterruptedly ever since the Federal Reserve started its procedure of using fiat money to convert government debt instruments into new reserve assets of the banking system some four decades ago.

In view of these realities, it is pertinent to raise the question of whether these procedures at the heart of the inflationary process violate the U.S. Constitution. Opponents of this position may claim that because the Constitution says nothing about inflation, the whole issue is irrelevant. Let us examine this argument. The Constitution is a compact between the people and the government. It gives certain powers to the latter to assure the common good. Having experienced years of tyrannical rule by a foreign government, the framers of the Constitution wanted to make sure that their own creation did not fall prey to similar tendencies. It was clearly the intention of the Constitution to protect citizens against arbitrary actions of their government that would deprive them of property. The specific nature of such deprivations was left out purposely, for good reasons—namely, to prevent the government from getting around the barrier by avoiding only the acts specified, leaving it free to engage in others. In effect, the government is prohibited from engaging in any procedures whatsoever that will deprive people of their property without due process of law. Therefore, the constitutional stipulations are relevant to inflation.

The federal government cannot claim that any gains it makes from inflation are fortuitous. It is inconceivable that government officials are unaware of the enormous advantages the government gains from inflation in terms of lower debt financing costs and in terms of higher income tax receipts. This process has been going on year after year for some four decades. Moreover, the government bears sole responsibility for instigating the inflation dynamics.

In addition to violating the rights of people, inflation jeopardizes the very essence of representative government. For all practical purposes, the Federal Reserve's operations have become a major source of revenue for the government and have removed incentives for financial discipline on the part of our elected representatives. The American people considered taxation without representation sufficiently intolerable to initiate the independence movement. Inflation is a contemporary version of this same phenomenon. Instead of openly arriving at taxes in accordance with constitutional provisions, the Federal Reserve's actions are not subject to the checks and balances of the political process; nor are they implemented with any concern for equity and fairness. Moreover, these procedures have enabled the government to carry on unpopular policies, such as the Vietnam war, involving the expenditure of billions of dollars year after year, without being subject to the discipline stemming from the people's control over money via tax bills that have to be passed in the Congress. This reliance on the hocus-pocus of Federal Reserve financial manipulations as a substitute for budget and tax policies openly evolved in line with democratic procedures violates both the letter and the spirit of the Constitution. If we want to survive as a democracy, we had better take appropriate steps to stop the inflation swindle.

The government should do everything possible to avoid reliance on inflation as a major source of revenue or as a substitute for financial responsibility in matters involving taxes, debts, or budgets. In the interest of national conciliation, those who have been damaged by the government's actions should forgive past transgressions in return for wholehearted commitment to constitutional procedures by all government officials from now on.

THE BUREAUCRACY'S
FINANCIAL NEUROSIS

A neurosis is a mental disease characterized by self-defeating behavior, compulsive and obsessional features, and a lack of genuine satisfaction from life. Traumatic experiences at an early age are generally regarded as the cause of neurosis.

Inflation partakes of all the characteristics described above. It perpetuates old problems that should have been solved long ago. It prevents a realistic assessment of the present. It rigidly adheres to established patterns of behavior, even though they have brought neither positive results nor genuine satisfactions. The traumatic experience which gave birth to this financial neurosis in contemporary America was the Great Depression of the 1930s.

Inflation is characterized by a self-feeding pattern. It leads to financial and economic distortions which cause a breakdown of functioning in the form of recession. To counteract the latter, the government engages in deficit financ-

79

ing, which activates the Federal Reserve's fiat money creation mechanism, which causes more inflation. Like a neurotic individual, the government tends to perpetuate the very environment that causes the neurosis. Any attempt to break out of this self-imposed neurotic confinement is resisted with great tenacity, as if the very life of the individual or governmental entity were at stake.

The Federal Reserve's Open Market Committee and its policy of converting government debt instruments into new reserve assets of the banking system via fiat money is at the heart of the inflation neurosis. Both the organization and its policies were New Deal creations. Under the emergency conditions prevailing in the 1930s the emphasis was on quick action, not on careful deliberation. Even a financial genius could not have developed a sound long-range program under those circumstances. The Federal Reserve, which had failed to use its powers to impose financial controls on the runaway stock market speculations of the 1920s was rewarded for its failure by being given additional powers over the economy.

This action may seem strange, but rewarding failure is more common in governmental realms than most people realize. Bureaucrats often rationalize their inadequate performance in terms of inadequate powers. The more they fail, the more additional powers they say they need. Moreover, bureaucrats have a propensity to define success or failure in terms of their own power position, not on the basis of results achieved for society. To a bureaucrat, anything that increases his power constitutes success, while anything that reduces his power is a failure. Thus, bureaucracy has a vested interest in maintaining policies that assure failure in terms of external function, for those policies will continue or even enhance their power. It follows that from the standpoint of the bureaucracy, any policy that promises a real solution to an existing problem like inflation constitutes a threat and may be resisted.

Like the sorcerer's apprentice who did not know how to stop, the Open Market Committee of the Federal Reserve has been flooding the economy with fiat funds on a scale that has made chronic inflation a fact of life for the past several decades. It is characteristic of neurotics to blame others for their misdeeds through a process known as projection. Favorite whipping boys include businesses which raise prices, and labor unions which demand higher wages. Increases in prices and wages are of course inevitable in an environment dominated by the chronic infusion of fiat funds, which compete with legitimate earnings and savings for goods and services. Whenever inflation heats up, the first solution that bureaucrats propose is control over wages and prices. The dynamics may be described as follows: Create a problem, such as inflation, by bureaucratic mismanagement; blame the victims for having caused the problem; provide a solution that increases your power at the expense of the victims, such as wage and price controls; and threaten the victims with dire consequences if the controls are removed.

Neurotics often embroil others in their problems. This provides cover and support for their behavior. The bureaucrats cleverly chose to implement their inflation-producing mechanism by involving the banking system in their scheme. Moreover, as their actions affect the whole economy, they can claim that any fundamental changes would have harmful consequences.

The inflation neurosis prevents genuine satisfaction. As people endeavor to deal with inflation's impact, they sooner or later find themselves victimized by it. Even the government risks eventual trouble for itself because of the uncontrolled inflation specter. Ultimately, no one gains from inflation except the enemies of democracy and of free enterprise.

How can one explain that the people who manage the nation's financial affairs seem to have fallen into this neurotic trap? Institutions tend to develop a life and rationale of their own, with a profound influence over all those involved in their affairs. A selective process tends to eliminate those who might cause trouble by questioning the premises on which the institution operates. Those who filter through this selection process will either adjust to the prevailing situation or will feel so unhappy that they leave.

The very fact that the institution has existed for a

long time and has followed certain procedures and policies generates a strong momentum for self-perpetuation. The sense of power that comes from controlling such an institution entails significant psychological rewards. Even the irrational and antisocial aspects of an enterprise may appeal to unconscious drives. Psychiatrists have found that some of the most moralistic people have deep-seated wishes to engage in immoral acts. Very few neurotic satisfactions can equal the ability to engage in illicit behavior in a socially sanctioned framework. Who can resist the temptation to engage in a kind of counterfeiting that appears to have the sanctions of law and institutional support on its side? Why worry about financial discipline when you can have the power of omnipotence, controlling fate with the money printing press?

Such dynamics go all the way back to early childhood, when the infant could control his environment (Mother) by opening his mouth and letting out a signal that he wanted something. The mere desire for food or comfort was usually instantly gratified. Few adults can achieve such results, though many try. The bureaucrats who run the Federal Reserve's Open Market Committee come closest to obtaining such instantaneous gratifications of their neurotic wishes. For example, if they want interest rates to decline, they just purchase enough government bonds with unlimited fiat funds until their goal is met. Nothing in the real world can withstand this power.

It is important to recognize these neurotic dynamics in dealing with the problem of inflation. Rational discourse and solutions can be easily defeated by such realities. The first step in the right direction is to know the truth, to start asking the right questions, to include as many dimensions of reality as possible. Then, perhaps there will be some mature, well-integrated personalities in positions of power whose ideas are compatible with those seeking to solve the problem of inflation. They can play a key role in helping us to overcome the inflation danger that threatens us all.

VICTIMS AND CULPRITS

Inflation's adverse impact on costs is universal, but its distribution of illicit gains is highly uneven. Those who benefit more than they lose from inflation have a vested stake in its continuation. Without doubt the federal government is the largest single beneficiary. Savers with their funds tied up in fixed-income accounts and securities whose return is below inflation rates are the main losers.

From the standpoint of the costs of goods and services, everybody feels the adverse impact of inflation. Individuals, associations, corporations, and governments have to increase their expenditures at least in line with inflation if they want to maintain existing levels of consumption. Any curtailment of expenditures below levels adjusted for inflation represents a sacrifice of living standards.

The federal government benefits from inflation because it is the largest borrower and because it collects income taxes on an ascending scale. With the federal debt approaching $700 billion, each 1 percent inflation not covered by interest rates represents a gain of $7 billion to the government. Inflation virtually guarantees such gains to the government, because the fiat funds which are responsible for inflation also depress interest rates. Some of the tax benefits from inflation include higher tax collections because of larger nominal incomes and taxing the inflation factor in interest rates. These, too, involve billions of dollars annually.

Other gainers from inflation include all those who can raise their income beyond the rate of inflation and improvement in productivity. Those in the best position to do so are governments with the power to enforce their will on the economy without fear of adverse economic, legal, political, or other consequences to themselves. Foreign rulers are in a particularly advantageous position in this respect.

The main victims of inflation are all those on fixed incomes whose return on savings is below the sum-total of taxes and inflation rates. For example, if interest income is 5 percent and the combined total of taxes and inflation is 10 percent, the net loss is 5 percent of the capital involved. These losses constitute a form of expropriation of property without due process of law. In effect, inflation represents a massive redistribution of property from the prudent sectors of society to the profligate spenders in our own government and to others who can emulate their behavior with impunity.

When the rate of inflation is 6 percent and productivity increases contributed by labor amount to 4 percent, labor is justified in seeking wage increases aggregating 10 percent. Such a labor agreement is not a cause of inflation, but a reflection of inflationary realities. Similarly, if a business raises its prices in line with increased costs, including the inflation adjustment, this is realistic behavior. However, if labor were to demand more than the figures cited, it would add to the inflationary distortions. The same is true of a business which raises its prices more than its costs, including inflation rates.

Most American labor unions and businesses have been remarkably restrained in their wage and price policies, considering the fact that inflation has plagued this country for some four decades and the temptation to use it as a cover for illicit gains must be great. The free enterprise system has given a good account of itself under very difficult circumstances. The same cannot be said of government bureaucrats and politicians, both here and abroad, many of whom have abused inflation for their own ulterior purposes.

History shows that in the long run inflation is a losing proposition for everybody, including governments. The latter will increasingly find that their inflationary procedures become less effective and arouse ever more resistance on the part of the population. People may not understand all the intricacies of high finance, but they can tell when they are being treated unfairly. A government that disregards the basic sentiment for fairness in its people courts serious trouble.

LABOR HAS A BIG STAKE

In the industrialized world workers have accumulated significant savings in the form of social security, pension plans, government savings bonds, savings accounts, and life insurance policies. Because all of these provide a fixed income, they are particularly vulnerable to the impact of inflation. Labor unions have paid insufficient attention to this area, in part at least because of illusory notions about the supposedly beneficial effects of inflation on employment.

During the 1930s the notion became widely accepted that monetary stimulation by the government would create more jobs. While this idea may have had some merit in a deflationary environment when the government itself was in sound financial shape, it is totally inapplicable at a time of chronic inflation and high governmental indebtedness. Under the conditions that have existed since World War II, inflation has in fact been the greatest single threat to labor, both in terms of undermining many of the financial gains it has achieved and by posing the ever-present risk of economic collapse.

This reality is clearly demonstrated by the experience during 1974 and 1975. In those two years the dollar lost one-fifth of its purchasing power. In the same period, unemployment reached over 9 percent of the labor force. Thus, workers lost a substantial part of their savings in real terms (purchasing power) while the unemployment lines were the longest since the 1930s. After this experience, no one can claim that inflation is beneficial to labor.

The Social Security system is the largest single owner of U.S. government securities. Most pension funds also have large investments in financial obligations of the U.S. government. Moreover, millions of individual workers purchase government savings bonds regularly. It is no exaggeration to say that workers have the largest stake in protecting government securities against the inroads of inflation. Labor unions should therefore play a leading role in putting pressure on the government to issue inflation-proof bonds. They should consider the battle for protecting workers' savings against inflation as important as their fight for decent working conditions and for improved wages.

In a democracy it is essential that the greatest possible number of people get involved in the political process to assure optimum results. Workers can make a major contribution to their own interests as well as to the common good by helping in the battle against inflation.

CORPORATE FINANCE MUST FOCUS ON SURVIVAL

If one made a survey of corporate executives and asked them about the primary objective of their businesses, they would undoubtedly place profits ahead of everything else. Under normal economic conditions this is an understandable and essentially correct assessment. If an enterprise is profitable, one may infer that it is fulfilling its economic function and that it is reasonably well managed. It follows from this scenario that the most important corporate document under such conditions is the profit and loss statement, which reflects all those items of current corporate performance that determine the profitability of the enterprise.

When inflation first appears on the scene, it gives the impression of improving the earnings picture. Sales and profits of most corporations increase as much as or even more than the rate of inflation, giving the misleading impression that there is no cause for concern. In fact, during this phase ownership participation in corporations in the form of stock certificates is considered one of the prime hedges against inflation. This is the period of booming stock markets, "hot" new equity issues, and a general environment of almost limitless optimism.

What this assessment overlooks is the effects of inflation on the corporate balance sheets. As we have demonstrated throughout this book, inflation is a disguised form of bankruptcy. Its true purpose is to reduce outstanding indebtedness in real terms by undermining the purchasing power of money. As long as this process is not clearly understood, it can provide the illusion of progress. But the cumulative effects of inflation on corporate realities are highly dangerous and may prove fatal in many instances. This is particularly true if corporations are not aware of the nature of their dilemma. The overwhelming objective of corporations in an inflationary environment must be survival; all else is secondary or irrelevant. A healthy balance sheet becomes far more important than a glowing profit and loss statement, particularly if the latter weakens the financial position of the corporation.

Let us examine some of the major balance sheet items in a typical corporate report and see how inflation affects them. Cash requirements invariably increase during inflationary periods. As everything costs more, additional cash is needed to pay current bills. In addition, inflation tends to distort economic and financial realities, creating unforeseen circumstances which generally require more cash.

Accounts receivable, which are normally considered near-cash items, become increasingly difficult to collect on time. For example, in a normal economic environment receivables are turned over within thirty days by most corporations. In an inflationary period the time interval might be stretched to sixty or more days. Moreover, corporations will have to spend additional sums to make these collections, such as the use of factors or other intermediaries. It should be noted that receivables represent that portion of sales for which proceeds have not been collected. If under normal circumstances they amount to about 10 percent of sales, during inflationary periods they may climb to as much as 25 percent of sales. The net effect is a substantial reduction in corporate liquidity. Ironically, under such conditions the greater the sales and reported profits, the more illiquid the corporation may become. A brilliant profit and loss statement could become a disastrous balance sheet.

Inventories, the other major near-cash items, also are seriously distorted by inflation. Invariably the valuation of inventories goes up during chronic inflation. As corporations use up these inventories, they report them as highly profitable sales on which they of course pay income taxes. This is particularly true when they use FIFO methods of accounting, in which the inventories bought first, normally at the lowest prices, are used to establish costs. This is a hangover from the days when corporations wanted to make their profit and loss statements look good so that investors would like their stock. Under inflationary conditions, this process benefits only the tax collector. It increases the drain on the corporate cash position, for taxes are liabilities that must be paid on time before anything else. While it may make the profit and loss statement look good for a while, it is deadly for the cash item on the balance sheet, representing a serious drain on liquidity.

A similar reduction of corporate liquidity is produced by the understatement of depreciation of property, plant, and equipment in terms of their replacement costs, leaving the corporation with inadequate sinking funds. This is particularly relevant to such companies whose fixed assets require continuous replacements or additions. It is almost universal experience that the cost of fixed assets during the current inflation has risen far more than the rate of inflation would indicate. In many cases their costs are twice as much as the general decline in purchasing power. Inflation in effect undermines the fixed-asset category, resulting in lower productive resources in real terms accompanied by higher taxes. The latter is due to the fact that depreciation, which is a deductible item for tax purposes, does not reflect the realities and therefore results in higher tax liabilities.

The sum total of these factors on the asset side of the balance sheet is a serious drain on corporate liquidity at a time when the need for such liquidity is higher than ever. The effects of these realities can be seen on the liabilities side. The most striking phenomenon concerns corporate indebtedness. In an inflationary environment, corporations are forced to go into ever deeper debt in order to take care of their financial requirements. Even the most impressive profit and loss statement does not compensate for the serious drain on cash due to higher taxes, delayed collection of receivables, and soaring fixed-asset replacement costs. Corporations that had hitherto prided themselves on the fact that they never borrowed in the bond market now come forth with record issues. Corporate borrowings have reached the highest levels in history, aggregating over $1 trillion. Moreover, much of this borrowing is done on terms that could seriously jeopardize corporate viability if we ever experienced a deflationary period. Already about half of all corporate pre-tax earnings are required for debt servicing; this is at a time of record reported earnings. If we ever got into a situation in which earnings were to decline drastically, interest costs could take up all earnings; in fact, there might not be enough earnings to cover interest.

It is clear from this assessment that the chronic inflationary environment that has prevailed during the past four decades has induced the corporate sector to push its financial resources to the limit. In many cases, this creates vulnerability to adverse developments. Those who want to assure their survival may be well advised to follow prudent financial policies, even if this involves sacrificing expansion and current operating performance. The primary focus should be on a viable balance sheet, one that can withstand the buffetting of economic storms resulting from inflationary distortions.

THE HAZARDOUS POSITION
OF LOCAL GOVERNMENTS

In the past twenty-five years the indebtedness of states
and local governments has risen with exceptional rapidity.
Such debts rose from $26 billion in 1950 to more than $200
billion in 1976. Increasingly, the financial resources of these
entities have been mortgaged to the future. Their expenses
have risen sharply in line with increased responsibilities,
long-term budgetary commitments, and inflation. Sharply
higher taxes have been insufficient to meet all these requirements. Borrowing has therefore been necessary to
close the gap.

When states and local governments raise funds,
they have to function within the framework of the free
market. Their only special feature is the tax-exempt status
of the interest on their securities. While this attracts many
investors, it has not prevented interest costs from more
than tripling since the 1940s, to almost 7 percent on the
highest grade tax-exempt bonds in 1975.

States and local governments are among the main

victims of inflation. Virtually all their expenditures go up at least in line with inflation, while a substantial part of their income is not equally secure. The federal government has given some recognition to the problem by instituting a policy of revenue sharing with the states. In effect, this means that a portion of the funds which the federal government has siphoned from the states through its escalating income taxes and inflation are returned to the states. While this is a step in the right direction, it does not deal with the fundamental problem.

The biggest contribution the federal government could make to the local governments would be to restore financial discipline to its own operations. This would be the most important step in bringing inflation under control. It would also curtail the federal government's unfair position in the capital markets. Finally, it would reduce unrealistic expectations on the part of the population as to the proper role of government.

Any reduction of inflation would be of direct benefit to the states and local governments. Since the federal government's financial irresponsibility is the primary cause of inflation, a reversal of that situation would be most helpful to the states. During the next several years, the federal government will be dominating the capital markets to an unprecedented degree. Its borrowing requirements will be so high that all other seekers of funds, including states and local governments, will have difficulty obtaining their share. In competing for funds, the federal government has unfair advantages over all others because it is operating outside the discipline of the free market. The U.S. Treasury and the Federal Reserve will make sure that the federal government gets its funds on its terms before anybody else is given consideration. The states, along with the private sector, are at the mercy of the powers in Washington.

Ever since the 1930s people have been led to believe that they can get something for nothing through government intervention. A pattern of rising expectations of government employees, welfare recipients, special-interest

The Hazardous Position of Local Governments

groups, and many others was set in motion. The states and local governments have felt the full impact of these expectations without being in a position to bail out their obligations through inflation, which has been Washington's prerogative. Moreover, their taxing and borrowing capabilities are close to realizable limits. They are reduced to being beggars asking for ever larger handouts from Washington.

What can the state and local governments do to restore their financial viability? They can use their political influence to make sure that the federal government moves in the direction of financial responsibility. Under the federal system of government, the states have constitutional rights and powers. The U.S. Congress is made up of delegates from the states. The governors of states and mayors of municipalities can exert considerable influence on behalf of their constituencies. Similarly, the political parties are based on local and state organizations. They can play a key role in influencing the federal government's policies. A curtailment of the financial irresponsibilities of the federal government would be in the best interests of the country. It is therefore a legitimate area for action by states.

Another intriguing suggestion to the states is to issue inflation-proof bonds. The procedure would be similar to that recommended for federal securities. From a practical standpoint, the federal government is going to delay issuing such bonds as long as possible, for they would in effect put the government back under the discipline of the marketplace. The states do not need to concern themselves with that problem, for they are already under such discipline. Moreover, as their securities are tax-exempt and as they would be presumably the first issuers of such bonds, they could put the fixed interest rates at the lowest levels in memory. There are so many investors concerned about inflation that an inflation-proof bond by a state with a high credit rating might be saleable in the 1–2 percent interest range. If enough states issued such bonds, it would put increasing pressure on the federal government to follow suit, thus accomplishing a major objective in the fight against inflation. In any case, it would give states an invaluable competitive edge in the battle for funds that is facing them. Such bond issues should be undertaken only after careful examination of the realities involved. The indentures should be drawn up in such a manner as to provide proper safeguards against extreme contingencies. The expertise involved, while complex, is not insurmountable. Some investment banking firms have already done preliminary work along these lines.

Many people tend to blame state and local governments for being contributors to inflation because of their escalating spending programs and large indebtedness. However, it is not spending or indebtedness by themselves that will cause inflation; it is the entity functioning outside the rules of the game of the financial market system which is the real culprit. Only the federal government has removed itself from outside discipline and manipulates money, credit, and interest rates in its favor. Recent events in the affairs of New York City highlight this distinction. After years of irresponsible financial actions, the city had to agree to all kinds of conditions in order to avoid open bankruptcy. By way of contrast, can anyone imagine a group of bankers telling the federal government how it has to cut back on services, personnel, and general operations if it wants to get any further loans? It is the absence of this external discipline which is the key to Washington's financial irresponsibility and the inflation that flows therefrom.

RECESSION IS NO CURE

When the New Deal brain trusters initiated monetary manipulations to stimulate the economy, they thought they had found the key to perpetual prosperity. History has shown them to be mistaken. The primary result of their policies was chronic inflation. Recessions and unemployment of increasing severity have plagued the economy. Faced with the realities of high inflation, the bureaucrats came up with the equally fallacious notion of stimulating recession to cure the inflation. In reality, the effects seem to be a combination of the worst features of high inflation and high unemployment. The solution to the dilemma is to move in the direction of getting the government out of the business of manipulating the economy for its own ulterior purposes.

      Under normal economic conditions, if the federal government had not interfered in the market economy, inflation would have been cured long ago. Historically, excessive general price levels characteristic of war periods were brought back to noninflationary levels by sharp economic declines of short duration. The recession of the early 1920s was the last example of this pattern.

The chronic inflation that has beset the United States since 1940 was not allowed to be brought under control by free-market forces. Each time the economy tried to rectify the excesses that had developed, the federal government stepped in to prevent this process from running its course. The cumulative effects of this federal intervention are such that a simple adjustment of general price levels through market forces is no longer possible. Moreover, the cost of federal intervention has climbed precipitously. The recession of the late 1950s involved federal deficits of about $15 billion; of the late 1960s, $37 billion; of the early 1970s, $60 billion. The current recession has already cost the government some $150 billion in deficits. Moreoever, these deficits seem increasingly to lose whatever effectiveness they may have had in stimulating the economy to full employment of resources. Each dollar of deficit generates a decreasing amount of gross national product.

The government's approach to recession is in a vicious cycle. The decreased responsiveness of the economy to federal stimulation requires ever higher amounts of deficit financing, which in turn spawns higher rates of inflation. To combat the latter, the government resorts to policies of restraint, which leads to more recession. In fact, what has emerged is a chronic pattern of recession combined with inflation. It is no longer a question of one or the other; rather, the issue seems to be how much of each evil we are willing to tolerate. Even this choice is likely to disappear as events unfold.

The distortions created by four decades of government intervention in the market economy account for the chronic inflation as well as the growing ineffectualness of the government's steps. By trying to substitute political and bureaucratic manipulations for the discipline of the marketplace, the government has left the economy in a weakened position.

Can the situation be rectified? There is still hope that this is possible with the right approach. The restoration of a sound currency must have top priority. A stable long-term standard of value must be established, not subject to governmental manipulations. Instead of trying to control the economy, the federal government should concentrate on straightening out its own financial affairs. Specific suggestions along these lines are given in Chapter 26, "Inflation Can Be Conquered."

To cite a practical example of what can be done by realistic policies to bring inflation under control while generating sound economic growth, the Brazilian experience may be enlightening. Between 1964 and 1973, the inflation rate in that country was reduced from over 100 percent per year to about 16 percent. Since 1967, the annual growth rate in real terms (adjusted for inflation) has averaged around 10 percent. The Brazilian government has restored soundness to its currency by virtually universal inflation-proofing of all long-term financial instruments. This has been combined with the institution of financially responsible government policies. Free enterprise has been allowed to flourish and all sectors of the economy have benefited from the real growth that has taken place. Our southern neighbor can teach us a great deal about how to cope with inflation without victimizing ourselves with self-defeating policies. A penetrating analysis of the Brazilian experience is provided by Professor Alexander Kafka's "Indexing for Inflation in Brazil," which appeared in *Essays on Inflation and Indexation* (American Enterprise Institute for Public Policy, Washington, D.C., 1974).

THE INFLATIONARY
DEBT SPIRAL

Inflation and debt reinforce each other. Fiat funds poured into the economy by the Federal Reserve encourage a pattern of living beyond one's means. "Spend now and pay later" becomes the guiding principle of governments, individuals, and corporations. Total indebtedness has risen to over $3 trillion (three thousand billion dollars). The ultimate outcome of this frantic borrowing spree is likely to be widespread bankruptcy in the private sector. The instigator of this pattern, the federal government, will end up controlling ever larger segments of the economy because of its money-creating monopoly.

The more fiat money is issued, the higher the debts will pyramid. In an inflationary environment, costs increase continually and internal funds become inadequate to finance requirements. As a result, an ever larger proportion of the population has to borrow to make ends meet. While the rate of inflation reduces the burden on the borrowers, this advantage is offset by the need to borrow ever more. Thus borrowers in the private sector may win some battles with inflation, but ultimately they will lose the war. Open bankruptcy will be the fate of many. The only one to gain from this pattern is the federal government, which has control over the money-creating mechanism. This fact will lead to ever more power for the federal government at the expense of everybody else, including local governments, corporations, labor unions, and individuals. Ultimately, ever more institutions will become wards of Washington. It is not too far-fetched to consider inflation as the harbinger of a society dominated by the central government.

Ironically, the financial institutions in the private sector facilitate conditions that may ultimately lead to widespread financial failures and threats to their own viability. The enormous quantities of fiat funds force-fed into the economy by the Federal Reserve induce the banks to use every possible device to encourage people to live beyond their means, to go into debt. Every tool of advertising and promotion is utilized to accustom people to the notion of "buy now, pay later." The profit performance of banks depends upon finding outlets for their funds in the form of loans and investments. An ominous spiral of debt generation has taken place which may be good for current profitability of banks, but may seriously undermine their balance sheets as ever more customers become overextended and unable to repay their debts. It took almost two hundred years for total indebtedness in the United States to reach one trillion dollars by 1962. Since that time, this amount has tripled, to more than $3 trillion in 1975 (*U.S. News & World Report*, November 17, 1975).

The very magnitude of the problem makes it difficult to take decisive action to bring it under control. The government's financial mismanagement has created a Frankenstein that jeopardizes everyone. If the Federal Reserve tries to stem the tide by tightening the money supply (for instance, by issuing fewer fiat funds), an economic recession quickly ensues, with widespread bankruptcies resulting among the increasingly marginal borrowers. Like an addict, the economy requires ever larger infusions of fiat funds just to keep functioning.

There is no quick or easy solution to this dilemma. We must be prepared to allow considerable time to restore a more viable financial environment. Ultimately, it will be found that the old values of hard work, thrift, prudence, and living within one's means are the only sound basis for running an economy and a country. They can be restored to their rightful place only if the federal government stops following self-serving inflationary policies.

JEOPARDIZING
THE SAVINGS FUNCTION

The efficient production and distribution of goods and services requires tools, factories, mines, power plants, transportation, communication, stores, and other means. In the aggregate, these instruments of production and distribution may be called the capital base. How does this capital come into existence? Basically, through the use of savings of funds from income that are not spent on current consumption. People are encouraged to save by paying them interest for the use of money which is thus released from current consumption. In other words, people can earn money by depriving themselves of the enjoyment of the goods and services which they might otherwise purchase. Savings are also the source of all loans. The savings mechanism is essential for the proper functioning of a dynamic economy.

In order to work properly, the savings mechanism must be based on a sound foundation. The saver must be assured that his money is safe, that his income is fair, and

Table IV

SAVINGS AND INFLATION

Year	Interest Rate %	Inflation Rate %	Difference % Positive	Negative
1940	2.00	0.96	1.04	
1941	2.00	5.00		3.00
1942	2.00	10.66		8.66
1943	2.00	6.15		4.15
1944	2.00	1.74	.26	
1945	2.00	2.28		.28
1946	2.00	8.53		6.53
1947	2.00	14.36		12.36
1948	2.00	7.77		5.77
1949	2.00	(0.97)	2.97	
1950	2.00	0.98	1.02	
1951	2.00	7.90		5.90
1952	2.50	2.18	.32	
1953	2.75	0.75	2.00	
1954	3.00	0.50	2.50	
1955	3.00	(0.38)	3.38	
1956	3.00	1.49	1.51	
1957	3.25	3.56		.31
1958	3.25	2.73	.52	
1959	3.50	0.81	2.69	
1960	3.75	1.60	2.15	
1961	3.75	1.01	2.74	
1962	4.25	1.11	3.14	
1963	4.25	1.21	3.04	
1964	4.40	1.31	3.09	
1965	4.40	1.72	2.68	
1966	5.00	2.86	2.14	
1967	5.00	2.88	2.12	
1968	5.00	4.20	.80	
1969	5.00	5.37		.37
1970	5.00	5.93		.93
1971	5.00	4.30	.70	
1972	5.00	3.30	1.70	
1973	5.25	6.23		.98
1974	5.25	10.97		5.72
1975	5.25	9.14		3.89
Totals			43.51	58.85

Sources:
Inflation rates were based on information supplied in *The Handbook of Basic Economic Statistics*, March 1976.
Interest rates on savings accounts were the maximum allowed rates cited in the *Savings Banks Fact Book*, Savings Banks Association of New York State, 1974.

that he is repaid in full when the term of his investment has expired. If these basic requirements are not met, the savings function will be jeopardized.

Table IV shows that savings have been seriously undermined by inflation. Between 1940 and 1975, savings accounts provided a cumulative *negative* yield of more than 15 percent because of inflation. Taxes of course add to these losses.

It is noteworthy that the losses were concentrated primarily in the period 1941–48 and again in 1973–75. The losses tended to be sizable, exceeding 5 percent per annum in six years, with a peak of 12.36 percent in 1947. Gains, on the other hand, were always modest, exceeding 3 percent only four times. Interest rates did not start climbing until the 1950s and have been essentially static during the past several years. It is apparent that savings accounts are particularly vulnerable to sudden sharp upsurges in inflation rates because interest rates have not been adjusted with sufficient speed or magnitude to offset such developments.

These facts have not gone unnoticed. Savers have become increasingly conscious of yield differentials between savings accounts and other financial instruments. When the latter reach levels above those provided by savings accounts, a substantial amount of switching takes place, depriving savings institutions of their funds. The governmental regulatory authorities try to counteract this by giving savings institutions the right to provide higher yields on longer term accounts and by trying to restrict the availability of competing instruments. For example, Treasury Bills must be purchased in minimum amounts of $5,000, preventing the smaller savers from acquiring them. This is of course gross discrimination against the people who should be given every possible opportunity to improve their lot. It is also a vivid illustration of the counterproductive results achieved when bureaucratic manipulations are substituted for the free market. It makes a mockery of the claims that inflation benefits the poor.

The solution to this problem is to return to freely

competitive interest rates, giving the savings institutions the right to determine their own rates. Simultaneously, they should have the right to decide what interest to charge on mortgages and other investments. Inflation-proofing of savings accounts, similar to the procedures described in connection with government bonds, is another option worthy of serious consideration. The savings function is too important for the survival of the free enterprise system to remain in bondage to the self-seeking manipulations of government bureaucrats.

THE MYTHOLOGY OF MONEY

For many people, money is imbued with the fiction of inviolability and other attributes of the divine. This view is a heritage from the past, when currency was issued by absolute monarchs who expected their subjects to treat it as an extension of their own divinity. Interestingly, the U.S. government continues this fiction from absolutist days by printing on its paper currency "In God We Trust" on one side and "This note is legal tender for all debts, public and private" on the other.

    In spite of over thirty years of chronic inflation, most people psychologically are still inclined to consider money as having a fixed value. It may be useful to paraphrase Gertrude Stein to bring home the reality that "a dollar is *not* a dollar is *not* a dollar is *not* a dollar." Legally, a strong case can be made that whenever two or more parties engage in a long-term contract involving money, they mean to deal in stable purchasing power units and not merely in numbers. Otherwise, all financial contracts in an inflationary environment would be nothing but inequitable, misleading documents. If one party loans out $10,000 to be repaid in ten years, he expects to get the full value in terms of purchasing power back, not merely a piece of paper that says $10,000. It is about time that the law catches up with the realities of life.

Lawyers and judges can play an important role in facilitating the implementation of the approaches to inflation-proofing recommended here. Indentures and other instruments defining the terms of long-term debt should clearly spell out that interest rates or par values (amounts stated on the face of the documents) are to be adjusted for any declines in the purchasing power of the currency during their lifetime.

The concept of inflation-proofing can be expanded to testamentary wills, divorce settlements, and other contracts between private parties. It should become general policy to point out to clients that inflation-proofing is available as a means for assuring the equity of long-term contracts. If any legislation is needed to achieve this objective, lawyers should take the lead in pressing for it.

To facilitate a more realistic understanding of money during inflation, perhaps the legend on the currency should be amended to read: "This note is legal tender for all debts, public and private, provided there has been no loss of purchasing power during the life of such debts." Alternatively and even more accurately, the legend might state: "Caution, I am merely a piece of paper which states that I am worth one dollar. It is up to you to make sure that in your long-term financial transactions you safeguard yourself against misconceptions about my true worth. I make no claims and assume no responsibility in this regard."

In connection with his recommendation that purchasing power units be used to assure stable standard of value for long-term financial transactions, Alfred Marshall specifically suggested that lawyers and judges should facilitate the broad adoption of this principle. Law is concerned with basic equity in the dealings of men with each

110

other. The present system of using currency as a long-term standard of value is grossly inequitable in an inflationary environment. Anyone who has loaned money on a long-term basis during the past thirty years can attest to this reality.

The sooner we rid ourselves of the blind faith in money, the better off we will be. Instead of becoming victimized by mythological hangovers from the past, let us realistically assess the situation and recognize that money is worth only what it purchases in real terms. To translate this fact into operational procedures, we have to link all long-term contracts to cost-of-living indexes or similar devices. This new approach to money is a key to overcoming the evils of inflation.

22

GOLD IS NOT THE ANSWER

Inflation results from government manipulations of the currency for its own ulterior purposes. This process can take place whether the currency consists of precious metals or of paper. The techniques employed may differ, but the results are the same. In each case of such currency manipulation, the government manages to reduce the load of its debts and/or to increase its income. The government's creditors, taxpayers, and savers in general are penalized by such currency manipulations. History shows that gold and other precious metal currencies provide no true protection against this process.

Adam Smith cited the experience of the Roman Republic, whose currency was a 12-ounce unit of copper called the *as*. Copper was a precious metal in Roman times. As a result of the heavy debts incurred by the Roman government in its wars with Carthage, this copper currency was devalued twice and ultimately became worthless.

Similarly, Alfred Marshall, one of the leading

nineteenth-century economists, pointed out that gold cannot fulfill the role of a stable standard of value because of fluctuations in its own price. He noted that the problem would not be solved by adding other precious metals, such as silver, to the currency. According to Marshall, the only way to maintain a stable standard of value for long-term financial transactions is to devise purchasing power units independent of the currency. Both Adam Smith and Alfred Marshall lived at times when England and most other countries used precious metals as currency. They are therefore talking from firsthand experience.

One of the main arguments made in favor of gold is that it has an intrinsic value. In actuality, there is nothing stable about this "intrinsic value." Whenever there has been a free market for gold, its price has fluctuated over time. This is due to the same forces that determine the price of any other commodity—namely, demand and supply. The demand for gold is to some extent determined by its commercial and industrial uses, such as in jewelry-making, dentistry, and some electronics applications. This represents a small part of the total demand. Moreover, in many cases substitutes could be used. If the price of gold were dependent solely upon these uses, it would sell at a fraction of its present price. The main demand factor is undoubtedly that of monetary substitute. The current price of gold is therefore largely dependent on the hopes or fears of speculators.

On the supply side, gold is mined like other metals. It is found in many parts of the globe, with commercial production concentrated in South Africa, the Soviet Union, Canada, and the United States. This raises the specter that if everyone went back to gold, the producers would in effect hold unprecedented financial power over the rest of the world. They could institute a form of exploitation for their own ulterior purposes. This is an unacceptable situation from both an economic and a political point of view.

Gold has several practical drawbacks as currency. It is unwieldy to carry around. At the official price, if one

were to carry $500 in the form of gold it would weigh about
3/4 of a pound. Over a period of time, gold loses some of its
weight due to abrasion, not to speak of a tendency throughout history for governments to meddle with its content,
purity, and measurements. Classical writers cite numerous
instances in which gold was alloyed with lesser metals, por-
tions of coins were deliberately chipped off, and other types
of fraud were practiced. If gold were made into currency
again, insecurity about its reliability, purity, and safety
would pose major problems.

Those who speculate in gold get no interest on their
holdings. In fact, they have to pay interest for the money
they borrow to purchase gold, or they lose the opportunity
to earn interest if they use money they already have. They
have to store it in a safe place, which costs money, as does
the insurance. It is apparent that not everything glitters
about gold.

The gold speculators are hoping that the governments of the world will once again embrace gold as the main
currency. In the process of doing so, governments would
presumably raise the price of gold to reflect inflationary
realities. This procedure would wipe out a large part of the
outstanding debts, enriching both governments and gold
speculators at the expense of everybody else. The governments' creditors and savers would be just as effectively
defrauded by a tenfold increase in the price of gold as they
would by a tenfold increase in the amount of paper currency. In other words, the gold speculators are not primarily interested in solving the inflation problem; they just
want to profit from it.

The recommendations made in Chapter 26 "Inflation Can Be Conquered," represent real solutions which
would benefit the whole economy. In contrast, a return to
gold is gimmickry from which only the speculators and governments would profit.

The whole record of history shows that the nature
of the currency is not the decisive factor in determining the
presence or absence of inflation. Over the thousands of

years during which gold and other precious metals were the currencies, the destruction of wealth through government manipulation was a recurrent theme. If governments engage in profligate behavior, they will destroy wealth whether the currencies are in the form of gold or paper. Contrariwise, if governments manage their affairs prudently without going into debt, there will be no incentive for inflation, and currencies will remain stable no matter what their form.

23

THE IMPORTANCE
OF STABLE STANDARDS
OF VALUE

A stable standard of value is essential for the normal functioning of the economic system. Otherwise, all long-term transactions are in constant jeopardy. The chronic inflation that has beset the U.S. economy during the past four decades illustrates this principle.

It may be helpful to examine why currencies have failed to provide such stable standards of value. A currency may be considered an index of purchasing power with only one unit of measurement. Such an index is an open invitation to manipulation and speculation. If it serves the interests of a powerful party such as the government, to structure the currency in a self-serving way, this will generally be done. Such is the case when the government is heavily in debt and is unable or unwilling to repay its creditors in full. Under such conditions, governments have always manipulated currencies in their favor, regardless of the nature of such currencies. In Chapter 22, "Gold Is Not the Answer," it was shown that governments manipulated gold currencies by arbitrary designation of their value, and by reducing the gold content of coins. To this may be added the prohibition against ownership of gold or gold currencies by their citizens.

Paper currencies lend themselves even more readily than precious metals to government manipulations. If the bureaucrats showed as much creativity in sound government finance as they have in currency manipulations our problems would soon be solved. The major technique developed by the Federal Reserve is to use fiat money to convert government debt into new reserve assets of the banking system. This process creates money and credit on a leveraged basis, and provides cover for what the government is doing. It is a much more subtle technique than openly devaluing gold. This disguise helps prevent citizens from knowing what is going on.

Alfred Marshall pointed out that currencies do not provide stable standards of value even if the government does not engage in manipulations. For example, throughout much of the period between 1815 and 1914 the free enterprise system flourished in England and the United States with minimal government interference. Nevertheless, there were violent boom and bust cycles throughout this period. According to Marshall, these were largely caused by widespread speculation in the private sector against the future value of currencies. These speculations were engaged in not only by speculators, but also by virtually all participants in the economic system. The absence of a tamper-proof stable standard of value in effect forces most people to become speculators. This necessity distorts the whole economic system, rewards speculation at the expense of service to the community, and undermines people's faith in their economic and political institutions.

To avoid this dilemma, an index for a stable, long-term standard of value should be widely representative of the food, clothing, shelter, energy, appliances, cars, etc. making up the average purchases of the general population. Let us assume that an index consisted of 100 such components. It would be very difficult for anyone, even the government, to distort all these components at the same time. This is in sharp contrast to what happens with currencies. For this very reason Alfred Marshall noted that even a crude index is vastly superior to any currency as a stable long-term standard of value.

It is about time that we learned this hundred-year-old lesson and applied it to our situation. Once we have implemented this approach, we will wonder how we ever got along without it. We will look back upon our current procedures as a form of economic barbarism that persisted much too long.

24

THE CASE FOR INFLATION-PROOFING

Alfred Marshall pointed out about a hundred years ago that money cannot fulfill the role of a standard of value for long-term financial obligations. The reason for this assessment is to be found in the changing purchasing power of money over time. As stability of value is the essential prerequisite of all financial agreements involving a significant time factor, he examined alternatives to money for this purpose. He reached the conclusion that a purchasing power unit or index, made up of representative goods and services, would be a practical solution. For example, if significant categories of food, shelter, clothing, and energy were used for determining such a purchasing power unit, all parties to the agreement would know that the money they received or paid out at the end of the contract would buy approximately as much as it did at the beginning. Conceptually, this purchasing power unit would be the basis for all procedures used in measuring purchasing power. Marshall noted that even a crude index of this type is vastly superior to gold,

121

silver, or any other form of currency in safeguarding the long-term stability of values.

The best-known purchasing power unit in this country is the Consumer Price Index. This was started at the time of World War I by the Bureau of Labor Statistics to help set wages for shipyard workers. It was subsequently expanded to include the cost of goods and services bought by average wage earners and clerical workers living in urban areas. These make up an estimated 45 percent of the total population. Recognizing that this group does not represent a broad enough sample for many purposes, the Bureau of Labor Statistics intends to start a new index labeled the "Consumer Price Index for All Urban Households" and representing the relevant data for some 80 percent of all Americans (*The New York Times*, July 28, 1974). The use of sophisticated sampling techniques and computerized equipment facilitates the speedy and accurate handling of data. Nevertheless, in a dynamic, innovative society with an ever-changing stream of goods and services, it should be acknowledged that a perfect index cannot be constructed. However, as Marshall noted, it is not necessary for an index to be perfect to perform its function quite adequately as compared with the present reliance on money. For example, as shown in Chapter 4, "Washington's Interest Rate Deception," had government bonds been linked to the Consumer Price Index, most of the loss in purchasing power of investors could have been avoided.

In terms of objectives, inflation-proofing may be viewed as a device designed (1) to remedy the effects of inflation on the savings function; (2) to restore fairness to the relationship between borrowers and lenders; and (3) to achieve a stable long-term standard of value.

The specific purpose of inflation-proofing is to protect savings from the onslaught of inflation. Those who criticize this approach maintain that this would be mere treatment of the symptom and would not stop inflation. In fact, so-called symptom treatment can have very significant consequences, particularly if relieving the symptom happens to be a matter of survival. For example, much of the practice of medicine falls into the category of symptom treatment, yet no one would say that it is therefore of no value. The savings function is vital to the survival of the free enterprise system. To safeguard it against inflation is therefore a perfectly valid procedure, even if there were no other ramifications.

The inflation-proofing procedure does not play favorites between borrowers and lenders. When the loan is repaid it will have the same purchasing power as when it was made. This is fully compatible with the free market, which is also impartial. The objections that are raised against this procedure by the borrowers, notably the government, are based on the unacceptable assumption that borrowers ought to be favored. This has indeed been the practice ever since the New Deal days. It is a major cause of the distortions in the economy, the irresponsibility of government, the overextended debt spiral, and the chronic inflation.

There is a further dimension to inflation-proofing which leads to the very core of the theory and practice of the free enterprise system. According to this analysis, protecting purchasing power against both inflation and deflation constitutes the key to developing a stable long-term standard of value. Its existence would fill the void left by currencies, which lend themselves to government manipulations and other distortions. Such a stable standard of value would facilitate the task of preventing the violent swings in the business cycle, which result in periodic booms and depressions. Alfred Marshall's approach to the problem was along these lines.

If an innovation serves to fulfill several important functions at the same time, it may be considered a basic breakthrough. I believe that inflation-proofing represents such a phenomenon. If properly applied, it should prove helpful in reducing the impact of inflation on savers, in stopping the distortions caused by deliberately favoring borrowers over lenders, and in providing the stable standard of value that will help prevent inflation, deflation, booms, and depressions.

Could inflation-proofing be accomplished by allowing interest rates to move freely in line with inflation rates? Unfortunately, that is impossible when the government deliberately manipulates the money supply in favor of borrowers. Experience has demonstrated that fiat funds interfere with the normal adjustment of interest rates. The fiat funds add to the supply of money, which brings interest rates down even though the reduced purchasing power would seem to call for higher interest rates. Thus, the normal functioning of interest rates is disturbed by the very dynamics of inflation.

It is a good idea to keep interest rates and inflation rates separate. Interest represents a rent on capital, while inflation is a destruction of capital. When one lumps them together, the issue is confused. The big spenders and borrowers can then complain about "high interest rates," when in actual fact it is the inflation rates which are high. The latter are of course caused by the government money manipulators themselves. Thus, inflation-proofing unmasks their endeavors to blame others for their own misdeeds. Furthermore, a separation of interest rates from inflation rates provides a foundation for a more equitable tax treatment. From the standpoint of fairness and justice, only the interest rate should be taxed, not the inflation rate.

Altogether, in a chronic inflationary environment, inflation-proofing is not merely desirable, but indispensable.

THE ETHICAL DIMENSION

All human conduct involves considerations of ethical values. The economic sphere is one of the most important areas of human interaction. To a large extent, it determines the material aspects of life. If an economic system is to function well, it is imperative that all participants be treated fairly and honestly. The free enterprise system operates on the premise that optimum economic goals are achieved if individual self-interest is harnessed to the common good. Historically, economists considered themselves to be teachers of applied moral philosophy.

In dealing with the problem of inflation, the ethical dimension is of primary concern. Inflation is a perversion of the normal function of money as a determinant of long-term standards of value. As this perversion permeates all facets of the economy, it increasingly undermines the normal functioning of economic processes. People recognize that something is wrong, and try to deal with it as best they can. In time, chronic inflation will lead to the collapse of faith in money and the economic system, with grave consequences for the whole society.

It is important to recognize that inflation is a human invention for dealing with a situation in which societies have lived beyond their means and are unable or unwilling to pay in full for the consequences of their action. In economics, as in all other spheres of life, there is no such thing as a free ride. Somebody always has to pay for value received. Payment may be postponed, but not avoided altogether. If it is partially or totally avoided by the recipient, then the payment was in effect made by those who provided the original funds for the services rendered. The creditors were thus defrauded of their money.

Society provides a regular procedure to take care of a situation created by an individual living beyond his means and unable to meet his obligations in full. Under these circumstances, he can turn to the courts and seek protection under the bankruptcy statutes. The courts then ascertain the assets and liabilities involved and decide on a fair distribution to all the creditors. The bankrupt is freed from the burden of his debt and can start a new life. This procedure has deep historical roots in Western civilization, going back thousands of years to the days of the Old Testament. The latter provides that once a year, on the Day of Atonement, human beings forgive each other their debts and gain divine forgiveness for their sins. Analogous procedures exist in other cultures also.

While individuals in the private sector of the economy have evolved this open bankruptcy procedure to fulfill a necessary function, governments have relied on manipulations of the currency to accomplish a similar objective. However, the very fact that this is a disguised procedure makes a big difference. It means that all kinds of confusion prevail as to what is involved and how to deal with it. In fact, it is a common practice of governments to blame the whole thing on the people, as if the creditors were guilty for having loaned the money in the first place.

Why don't governments declare themselves openly

bankrupt when they cannot meet their obligations? Here, too, we find historical roots. Throughout history, governments have generally considered themselves to be beyond the scope of normal behavior and rules of conduct. Rulers have regarded themselves to be in a class with gods who are not subject to human control. Governments make and enforce the laws and tend to claim control of everything and everybody, including, ultimately, all the wealth in the country. When they get into financial trouble, they proclaim it to be the people's fault. In any case, they have no compunction about taking wealth away from their subjects to meet their financial requirements. From this vantage point, inflation may be considered a seemingly more painless way of making people pay for government expenditures than alternative means, such as taxes. The government is like a debtor who can force all of his creditors to take less than they are owed without even thanking them for the favor. From a moral and practical standpoint, higher taxes would be far preferable to the deceptive procedure of inflation, for people could then recognize what is going on and have the satisfaction of being treated honestly and fairly.

While the saver suffers, the profligate governmental spender lives in a state of euphoria. He sees virtually no limit to what he can do to rescue himself and the world from all sorts of troubles by spending money on pet projects, and by managing the economy in the way he feels best. The analogy to the private sector would be that the bankrupt debtor not only causes losses to his creditors, but arrogates to himself the role of telling them how they should run their businesses. The result of such a procedure would inevitably be universal bankruptcy. This is the great risk involved in inflation.

Mature ethical conduct requires that everyone assumes responsibility for his behavior. In a democracy, this applies as much to governments as it does to individuals. It is imperative that we approach the task of overcoming inflation within this framework.

127

INFLATION CAN BE CONQUERED

A stable currency is a prime prerequisite to a well-functioning society. The conquest of inflation is imperative to restore soundness to our financial structures and economy. The American people are entitled to live free from the specter of inflation.

The most important step in conquering inflation is to remove all incentives from the government for causing it. These incentives fall into two categories: (1) power over the economy; (2) direct financial gains to the government.

The use of fiat funds to convert government debt instruments into new reserve assets of the banking system is an inappropriate tool for long-range economic policy. It was specifically designed to cope with conditions prevailing at the time of the Great Depression in the 1930s. Its use during World War II and thereafter was largely counter-productive. It generated all kinds of distortions, including inflation. It would be far more constructive if the government concentrated its efforts on straightening out its own

129

financial mess rather than adding insult to injury by manipulating the private sector. One of the reasons the government places so much emphasis on its supposed indispensability to the private sector may well be that such a role provides a good cover for its own large gains from this endeavor. The facts show that the government has not achieved its lofty economic goals of permanent prosperity and full employment. In the process of fostering popular delusions about perpetual good times, it has undermined the financial structure. In effect, it has added a disguised form of chronic national bankruptcy, namely inflation, to other unsolved problems.

The government's financial gains from inflation include interest rates below inflation rates plus a normal return on capital, debt repayment with depreciated dollars, higher income tax receipts, and freedom from financial discipline. The hundreds of billions of fiat dollars that have been poured into the economy by the government have systematically depressed interest rates, keeping them below normal rates of return, including inflation protection. Similarly, these fiat funds have enabled the government to repay its debts with depreciated dollars. These same fiat funds have generated increased nominal incomes, which are taxed at ever higher rates even though the real incomes, adjusted for inflation, have risen much less proportionately.

While these specific financial gains alone would provide the government with a strong incentive to continue inflationary procedures, there are other dimensions of great significance. The Federal Reserve's financial manipulations have placed the government outside the rules of the game of the free-market system. As a result, it need not concern itself with such ordinary problems as balancing the budget or limiting its propensity for profligacy. In fact, it can gain all the prerogatives characteristic of absolute monarchies. In the process, the unconstitutional and undemocratic nature of this procedure is conveniently overlooked.

The following procedures are designed to remove

most financial incentives for causing inflation from the government. Their implementation over a period of time will go far in bringing inflation under control.

1. All bureaucratic manipulation of interest rates should be terminated as soon as possible. This includes so-called open market operations of the Federal Reserve as well as all interest rate ceilings on savings accounts. Simultaneously, control over mortgage rates should be removed.

2. The government should give its creditors the option to acquire inflation-proof securities.

3. Income tax rates should be adjusted for inflation rates.

4. The Federal Reserve's powers over the money supply and the creation of fiat funds should be curbed. New procedures should be evolved to assure responsible management of this critical area. The avoidance of inflationary pressures should be given top priority.

5. The portfolio of government securities held by the Federal Reserve should be turned over to the U.S. Treasury to be canceled. This will prevent possible future mischief with these securities.

For the past four decades the bureaucrats have manipulated interest rates in favor of borrowers, notably the government itself. This is the very antithesis of the free market, which plays no favorites between lenders and borrowers. The significance of this factor can hardly be overestimated. Without free interest rates, resources are misallocated, the savings function is jeopardized, and financial discipline is undermined. The restoration of interest rates free from self-serving government manipulations should be a primary goal in the fight against inflation.

The issuance of inflation-proof securities by the government should be initiated at the earliest opportunity. This procedure can facilitate a more rational approach to the debt structure, including lower costs, lengthened maturities, and stronger incentives to save and invest. Such securities also provide incentives for the government to reduce inflation, for the lower the inflation rates, the lower the government's payout. Another advantage of inflation-proof securities is that they will allow the government time in which to implement other steps in the direction of a normalized economy.

The adjustment of income taxes to inflation rates is long overdue. It is intolerable that citizens should be forced to pay higher tax rates because of inflation that is caused by their own government. A thorough examination of all provisions of the income tax laws should be undertaken to make sure that inflation adjustments are applied wherever necessary to restore fairness.

The above recommendations with regard to interest rates, government debt issues, and income taxes will largely defuse the inflation problem, for they will remove from the government most direct financial incentives for fostering inflation. As these are implemented, a more rational approach to the issuance of new money can be established. The sole purpose of such new funds will be to help promote general price stability. Rather than adding haphazardly and in a manipulative fashion, a reasonable figure can be determined in line with national objectives but without favoring borrowers or profligate spenders, notably the federal government. This matter is so important that the Congress should have a direct hand in determining the amounts involved, with proper emphasis on the constitutional rights of all citizens, including savers.

This approach will greatly curtail the functions of the Federal Reserve's Open Market Committee. The latter should be restricted to taking care of seasonal and other temporary requirements of the banking system. As a further step in normalizing the government's financial structure, the federal debt securities currently held by the Federal Reserve should be presented to the U.S. Treasury for liquidation. In terms of the national balance sheet, such a transaction would have no substantive consequences. It is illogical for the Federal Reserve to be a creditor to the U.S. Treasury, as they are both parts of the same government. The liquidation of these securities would prevent the possibility of their misuse in the future, and would provide a clearer picture of the Treasury's debt position.

The overall effect of this package would be a considerable simplification of procedures with regard to money supply, interest rates, government debt, and income taxes. The government would lose virtually all incentives for causing inflation. The relationship between savers and spenders, lenders and borrowers, would be restored to one of impartiality, with free-market forces determining their terms of contract. The Federal Reserve could concentrate on supervising the banking system and related matters, without being burdened with the task of masterminding the whole economy. The biggest losers would be the politicians and the bureaucrats, whose powers would be curbed and who would be forced to practice financial discipline in carrying on the affairs of state. The biggest gainers would be the American people, who for the first time in decades would live in an environment that was freed from the specter of inflation.

While the implementation of this anti-inflation program should proceed as quickly as possible, the legacy of distortions caused by four decades of financial mismanagement by the government cannot be disregarded. Good will, patience, and persistence will be required. Since the government's income from inflation will be largely eliminated, some tax increases will be necessary while the politicians and bureaucrats adjust to lower levels of spending. Similarly, the pattern of living beyond one's means, translated into debts of some $3 trillion, requires gradual decompression. None of this will be easy, but ways can be found to move in the right direction. The issuance of inflation-proof securities will facilitate the transitional phase, for it will provide time and incentives for bringing inflation under control without penalizing either debtors or creditors. Good will and forgiveness for past transgressions should motivate all of us to achieve the desired objectives.

INFLATION-PROOF GOVERNMENT SECURITIES

The issuance of inflation-proof securities by the federal government should have top priority. This procedure would restore equity to its debt-financing operations. It would provide a maximum incentive for reducing inflation. Moreover, it would have several advantages for the government, including lower current interest costs, lengthened debt maturities, and time to restore financial soundness.

As was shown in Chapter 4, "Washington's Interest Rate Deception," the government's creditors have been treated unfairly over the past several decades. Interest rates have not provided a normal return on capital plus inflation protection. The government's infusion of fiat funds into the economy on a massive scale has caused both depressed interest rates and chronic inflation. The issuance of inflation-proof securities would rectify this situation.

As an increasing proportion of the government's debt becomes inflation-proofed, the incentive to take all possible steps to reduce inflation will be enhanced, for the lower the inflation rate, the less the government will have to pay out. This is in marked contrast to the present situation, which provides the government with a direct benefit from inflation. On ordinary government securities, such as those already outstanding, the higher the rates of inflation, the more financial gains the government achieves.

While the government would give up the inflation benefits, it would obtain other advantages. Current interest costs would be reduced. Its cash position would be enhanced. For example, contrast an 8 percent straight bond with a 3 percent inflation-proofed one. In the case of the former, the government will have only $920 per $1,000 bond at the end of the first year, while it will have $970 of the latter. In other words, the saving is not merely in interest costs, but in use of capital. Once the inflation specter is removed, investors' willingness to make funds available to the government at low rates for long periods of time will be greatly enhanced. Lengthening of the government debt is imperative, for the average maturity has fallen to less than two and a half years. Finally, the government would avoid locking itself into high interest rates, which partially reflect inflation rates. All of these advantages to the government could be achieved without penalizing its creditors and without providing any incentives for continuing inflationary policies.

The following example illustrates the procedures involved in issuing an inflation-proof bond. Let us assume that the government issues a ten-year bond with a par value of $1,000 and an annual interest coupon of 3 percent. At the end of each year, the government would calculate the rate of inflation or deflation during the preceding twelve months and adjust the par value accordingly. If the rate of inflation during the first year was 5 percent, then the adjusted par value would be $1,050. The 3 percent interest is then calculated on that basis, providing investors with a payment of $31.50 per bond. In contrast, if there has been a 5 percent rate of deflation, the adjusted par value would be $950 and the interest payment $28.50 per bond.

At the end of the ten-year term, the cumulative rates of inflation and deflation would determine the final settlement. For example, if the cumulative inflation rates amounted to 50 percent, then each bondholder would get $1,500 for each bond and the final interest payment would be $45. The important point to remember is that the investors would in effect have a guaranty that the money they make available to the government when they purchase the bonds will have the same purchasing power ten years from now, no matter what the intervening rate of inflation or deflation.

The attractiveness of these bonds would of course depend on the overall financial environment. If all the recommendations made in Chaper 26, "Inflation Can Be Conquered," are quickly implemented, the appeal of inflation-proof bonds would be quite limited. One the other hand, if inflation-proofing is the only procedure accepted, then its function may indeed be essential for financial survival.

The investment community should welcome inflation-proof securities, for they would be a new financial medium with great potential. The dynamics of inflation-proof bonds are the opposite of those of straight bonds. The former will rise as inflation increases and will fall as inflation declines. This is in contrast to straight bonds, which decline with increased inflation and rise with declines in inflation rates. Should we once again experience double-digit inflation, the long-term market for straight bonds may practically wither away while that for inflation-proof securities would flourish.

The issuance of inflation-proof securities by the U.S. government is one of the most constructive steps that could be taken on the road to conquering inflation.

TAXATION VERSUS INFLATION

In many respects, inflation has become a substitute for taxation as a major source of revenue for the federal government. Inflation enables the government to repay its debts with depreciated dollars, to depress interest rates and thus benefit its borrowing costs, and to increase its income tax receipts. The total amounts involved vary with inflation rates, and have averaged tens of billions of dollars annually in recent years. If the government were deprived of these inflationary subsidies, it would be forced to find other sources of revenue or to curtail its spending.

Nobody likes increased taxes. However, if the choice is between inflation and taxes, all responsible citizens should choose the latter. Taxes may be painful, but they are openly arrived at by means of democratic procedures within the framework of the U.S. Constitution. They reveal the true state of affairs, without deception or distortions. Everyone involved knows where he stands in relation to taxes. They constitute a rational tool for providing the government with income to take care of expenses. Moreover, the very reality of tax increases will cause the most critical examination of all expenditures, with far greater impact on realistic budget procedures than anything witnessed in recent decades.

In contrast to taxes, inflation is deceptive and employs procedures that are contrary to the letter and spirit of the Constitution. It masks the true state of affairs and provides the profligate spenders in government with a virtually free hand. Inflation distorts economic realities, undermines the financial stability of the private sector, and could ultimately lead to the destruction of the free enterprise system. Inflation contravenes all principles of sound finance and provides the government with the incentive to move ever deeper into a morass of higher deficits, larger debts, and greater irresponsibility.

The American people have a right to make their own decisions in this crucial area, rather than leaving the matter in the hands of bureaucrats and politicians who have deceived them all these years. The inflation swindle can be eliminated within a reasonable period of time if appropriate measures are taken. One of the necessary steps, at least on an interim basis, may be increased taxes. This is a small price to pay for ridding the country of one of its gravest threats.

This rational approach to taxes versus inflation will help lay the foundation for restoring realism to the government's procedures and policies. The government will have to give up its endeavors to be all things to all men. At the same time, it will enhance the government's ability to safeguard the vital interests of the American people with appropriate means, rather than relying on illusory notions that reflect inflationary self-deceptions.

WHAT INDIVIDUALS CAN DO

Inflation represents a breakdown of the normal rules of the game of the monetary system. The cumulative effect of the government's manipulations of money, credit, and interest rates for its own advantage is to put all other sectors of the economy into increasing jeopardy. Financial instruments are undermined, savings are eroded, and markets are distorted by this process. This monetary malady will also cause general disorientation, leading to confused behavior. It is a dangerous disease that could destroy society.

What can the individual do to protect himself against this threat? The most important prerequisite to correct action is to understand as fully as possible the nature of the problem. According to the analysis presented in this book, inflation is a disguised form of national bankruptcy caused by the federal government's financial irresponsibility. It is therefore imperative that all concerned citizens exert every possible pressure to rectify the situation. Those who run for public office must pledge themselves to place major emphasis on this issue if they want to get elected. The restoration of financial solvency must have top priority if we want to safeguard free enterprise and democracy.

Can the individual outwit the inflation game, and even profit from it? Quite frankly, we have not discovered any panacea. So-called inflation hedges contain traps. The dice are heavily loaded in favor of the perpetrator of inflation; all of us are suckers in a game that does not give us a real change. My first suggestion is active participation in the political process to help straighten out the financial mess in Washington. The other general recommendation to individuals is to make themselves as independent of the financial system as possible.

I do not propose to give anything resembling investment advice, as this book deals only with inflation and does not include the many other factors that have to be taken into account before making any investment decisions. The sole purpose of the ideas presented in the following pages is to stimulate thinking about inflation to improve the individual's chance to deal with it intelligently. The prudent procedure is to think carefully about your situation and to discuss it with members of your family, your attorney, accountant, banker, and other people whose judgment you trust.

PART I: SELF-MOBILIZATION

1. Consider putting your own house in order. Inflation creates a false sense of values about financial realities. It tends to encourage living beyond one's means by heavy borrowing. You should realize that in an economic downturn which could follow chronic inflation such debts could become difficult to manage. It may therefore be prudent to use periods of good income to reduce indebtedness. Loans with the highest interest rates should of course be eliminated first. Long-term mortgages with low interest rates

can be left alone, as long as you make sure to have sufficient financial resources to pay for the other expenses of the house under adverse conditions. Look over your assets carefully and figure out what is essential to your life and what is not. If you have debts, try to sell whatever is nonessential while prices are still high and pay off the debts. Some people may object to reducing indebtedness while the prospect of increased inflation is with us. They may of course be right, but on the other hand nobody knows when the game will be over. Moreover, while the general rate of inflation may increase, the particular assets you have may not benefit from that. Mass-produced items such as clothing, furniture, appliances, cars and boats are unlikely to increase in value once they are used. In any case, we are not trying to outsmart the system; we are merely endeavoring to survive a possible holocaust.

2. Invest in yourself. This is a good time to start learning new skills, improving your education, broadening your horizon by diversifying your job-related potential. Further on we shall cite some occupations that are likely to provide job opportunities even in a depression economy, and we shall also list some fields that are best avoided. The broader your range of skills and interests, the better your chance of weathering the storm with reduced hazard to you and your family.

3. Increase your self-sufficiency. Under the conditions envisaged here, earning money will be very difficult. The less dependent you are on money income, the better off you will be. If you can grow and prepare your own food, make repairs of home and equipment, sew clothes, and develop similar skills, you will be gaining independence. Moreover, such endeavors will have other significant advantages. You will have worthwhile things to do at home and avoid the frustrations that come from being dependent on others. Your self-sufficiency skills may even find a market with others and may lead to a new career for you. Incidentally, your nutrition and the quality of your life may actually be improved by this greater self-reliance.

4. Involve yourself politically. The situation facing us today is the greatest challenge to the American genius for self-government. If enough people get aroused about inflation and demand the right kind of action from their government, the miracle of subduing this disease without catastrophe might actually be accomplished. This would be the first time in history that this has been done, but there is no reason for not trying. Get together with other people and join in the battle against inflation. Both political parties need an infusion of inflation fighters. Join their ranks and make yourself heard. Make clear to candidates for public office that if they want your support, they must join the fight against inflation. As a test of their sincerity, check their views on the federal budget and the issuance of inflation-proof securities by the U.S. Treasury. The savers of this country and investors in government bonds have the right to demand protection from inflation. Translate this demand into political reality and you will have dealt a serious blow to the inflation swindle.

5. Include the inflation factor in investment decisions. It should be pointed out again that inflation is only one of the elements in the complex process of reaching a decision about investments. We must avoid the mistake of forgetting everything else. With these qualifications, we may proceed. Inflation distorts financial markets and can lead to costly mistakes. We have not discovered any investment that provides reliable protection from inflation. All the categories we have investigated contain traps for the unwary.

The impact of inflation on investments is most visible in the bond market. As has been noted, the government has followed a systematic policy of manipulating interest rates in favor of borrowers, with devastating effects on bondholders. Whenever interest rates are less than inflation rates and a normal return on capital, bondholders will suffer. This is such a clear-cut case that bondholder protective committees should be formed to tackle this fraudulent practice head-on. If present trends continue much longer, it would not be surprising if the bond market ceases to be a viable entity.

What was said about bonds applies equally to all fixed-income investments, including savings accounts, life insurance policies, and pension fund participations. To provide realistic protection of purchasing power, these entities should be inflation-proofed by linking their return to the cost-of-living index. It is self-evident that this can be done only if the income of these financial intermediaries is allowed fully to reflect inflation rates as well. Unfortunately, most politicians and government bureaucrats lack sound perspective on financial realities. In their ignorance, they would rather let the financial system suffer than give up a political advantage. In any case, savers should unite and press for action to have their funds protected from inflation. If enough people insist on inflation protection of savings as the issue with top political priority, politicians may find it to their advantage to champion this cause.

Stock prices are determined by many factors, of which inflation is only one. Whenever the Federal Reserve pushes for low interest rates by issuing increased fiat money and credit, the stock market is helped. This pattern gives rise to the notion that the stock market benefits from inflation. Contrariwise, when the Federal Reserve tries to counteract inflation by tightening the monetary reins and letting interest rates rise, the stock market tends to decline. As the chronic inflationary pattern unfolds, these dynamics may change. In advanced stages of inflation it is quite conceivable that double-digit inflation will accompany double-digit unemployment and major recession. What will the Federal Reserve do under those circumstances and how will that action affect the stock market? We do not pretend to have the answers to these and other questions. One general comment seems to be in order: Chronic inflation makes it increasingly difficult to reach realistic conclusions about the stock market. There will undoubtedly be violent swings, both up and down. But anyone who thinks he can ride out inflation by stock market investments is probably chasing after an illusion.

Real estate is often considered a hedge against inflation. Like stocks, this may work for a while, but if inflation goes on long enough the premises underlying real estate investments are increasingly undermined. The following tale is instructive. An investor had put his savings into strategically situated real estate properties in London. The value of these properties increased steadily as new office buildings were put up in their vicinity. It was the investor's hope that some syndicate would buy him out at a large profit. Unfortunately, the opportunity did not materialize in time. The building boom became a victim of the general stagflation gripping Britain. In the meantime his taxes, fuel bills, and other costs have skyrocketed, while his income from the rent-controlled properties has not kept pace. In fact, some tenants are unable to pay their rent in full and he cannot evict them because of government regulations. The inflationary environment turned a promising investment into a disaster. While this may be an extreme case, the pattern it depicts is applicable to many situations. Real estate investment is no sure hedge against inflation.

People who bought gold when it first became legal again in the United States have had some second thoughts about its supposed protection against inflation. The 1975 decline in the free market price of gold was as sharp as that of many stocks in the 1974 bear market. Those who have placed their faith in gold and other precious metals as the only "true" currencies immune to government tampering have not read history well. Indeed, most inflations in history prior to the twentieth century took place with precious metals as official currencies. Adam Smith cites many examples of such government manipulations of precious metals: by arbitrarily devaluing their content, by mixing lesser metals with them, by clipping coins, and by other fraudulent means. When governments are heavily in debt and are unable or unwilling to meet their obligations, they will find ways of defrauding their creditors no matter what the nature of the currency. Discipline and honesty of politicians are functions of character and institutional safeguards; they are not inherent in any substance that may be designated as money. It would be wonderful if we could wipe out inflation by making all governments return to gold as currency, but there is no financial or historical basis for this notion. Moreover, anyone entering the gold market should be aware of its lopsided nature on the supply side. Governments alone hold over one billion ounces of the metal; they can disrupt the price any time it suits their purpose. Gold production is concentrated in a few countries, some of which may have to sell their output to take care of financial needs. In any case, the historical record clearly shows that gold is no guaranteed inflation hedge. The same is true of silver and other precious metals.

Commodities rise and fall primarily in line with industrial demand and supply factors. While inflationary expectations may drive prices up, these lofty levels will not be sustained if there is a general decline in business, leading to lower demand from those who actually use the materials in their production. Speculation in commodities is a highly specialized skill that had better be left to professionals.

Fine art, antiques, and other valuables are often purchased in part as hedges against inflation. As a result, prices of many better known items have skyrocketed. This is a phenomenon typical of most such overpriced items; they go up in price because of the general belief that they are immune to inflation. This immunity, however, is strictly a function of belief, not reality. As inflation undermines the economic structure and an increasing number of people, including the purchasers of art, lose part of their wealth, the art market can be just as vulnerable as the stock market to serious price declines.

Foreign currencies and bank accounts have also been used by many people as possible havens from inflation. In reality, inflation is a worldwide phenomenon. Moreover, the economic distortions caused by inflation can

147

undermine the value of currencies even of countries adhering to conservative financial policies. For example, price gouging by the oil cartel has had adverse effects on the financial situation of Switzerland, which must import every drop of oil it uses. Interest payments on Swiss savings accounts to foreigners have usually been below the rate of inflation in Switzerland. Depositors in Swiss banks therefore are not protected from inflation; in fact, they may do worse than they would in the United States. Moreover, the average individual is better off having his funds close to home, so that he can take quick action to protect himself against adverse developments.

6. In connection with financial investments, emphasize safety, liquidity, and return on capital, in that order of importance. This should be done even if it means taking losses from chronic inflation. As inflation undermines the monetary and economic structure, an increasing number of entities may be faced with open bankruptcy. Under such conditions, safety of capital must have top priority. It makes little sense to get a high yield on a security when the capital itself may be wiped out. Under present circumstances, U.S. Treasury Bills provide the closest approximation to maximum safety and liquidity. Their yield of course does not protect against inflation. Moreover, we have no illusions about the financial solvency of the U.S. government. From a strictly pragmatic point of view, as long as the government has control over the monetary function and as long as any financial wealth remains in this country, U.S. Treasury bills will be reasonably safe. When they become worthless, all other financial instruments are likely to be without value, too.

It is disheartening to go through a list of investment alternatives and to find that for one reason or another all of them fail to provide genuine protection from inflation. The conclusion that U.S. Treasury bills are the only vehicle for trying to weather the storm is hardly inspiring. It should help to emphasize the point that inflation is an insidious disease that does not allow real protection to an individual's savings. The problem must be tackled directly through political means, to force the government to return to financial orthodoxy and constitutional procedures. Our main energies as responsible citizens should be directed to that task, rather than being dissipated on fruitless endeavors to outwit inflation.

PART II: THE EMPLOYMENT SITUATION

Chronic inflation inevitably generates ever-widening financial and economic dislocations, with massive unemployment one of its most painful manifestations. While job opportunities in general will decline, some sectors of the economy will fare better than others. Here are some of the fields of activity that are likely to provide job opportunities in an environment characterized by severe inflation and recession.

    1. Expertise in the bankruptcy field. Lawyers are likely to have a field day as the economy heads into troubled waters. Bankruptcy may become one of the dominant forms of business activity. In addition to lawyers, this will provide opportunities for a variety of specialists in liquidation, such as auctioneers, accountants, used-equipment dealers, and their staffs. A secretary working for a law firm is likely to have more job security than one with a bank or corporation, though of course this would not apply in every case.

    2. Public order and security operations. A depression will in all likelihood precipitate unrest and disorder on a large scale. The authorities will be hard-pressed to maintain law and order under these circumstances. Police, armed forces, and private security operators will play an important role in this endeavor. A career in the army or police is reasonably secure under most circumstances and with the influx of new recruits likely under depression conditions, career people have a good chance for advancement.

    3. Essential services, such as fire departments,

mass transit, public assistance and welfare. Firemen will be affected by the same factors as the police and armed forces. Welfare specialists, social workers, psychologists, and similar professionals will probably be in demand to take care of the many new cases seeking public assistance. As more people give up cars and use public transportation, job opportunities with subways, bus lines, and commuter railroads are likely to increase.

4. **Inexpensive forms of recreation and self-improvement.** Under depression conditions, people will turn to recreational activities that involve minimal expense. They will seek to use free time for additional training or for supplementing their income. Such hobbies as gardening, sewing, handicrafts, bicycling, and hiking will probably flourish. Adult education, job training programs, and counseling services will be in high demand. There will be increased reading of books, particularly those providing information on how to improve one's life. Fiction and other forms of literature enabling the reader to escape the harsh realities of life will also find good markets.

5. **Religious services.** Under adverse conditions, human beings tend to turn to religion for solace. There is likely to be a considerable increase in church attendance and participation in religious affairs. Many more people will join religious orders. Churches can provide many services in times of need.

6. **Political activity.** There will be a sharp increase in political activism. Existing parties will get an infusion of new members and additional parties may be formed. Demands for radical action to cope with the emergency will be heard on many sides. Totalitarian solutions will find new adherents. Political movements providing opportunities for jobs and status will gain momentum. Politics may replace economics as the main focus of attention.

7. **Health-related services.** When people have little to do and many things to worry about, the need for medical and psychiatric services is likely to increase. On the negative side, the inability of many people to pay high fees will

restrict medical income in comparison with periods of prosperity. High-cost medical services, such as elective surgery, will be in lower demand. Agitation for some form of socialized medicine will become stronger. Nevertheless, doctors will have no worry about work or sufficient income to put them in a relatively good position. The same applies to nurses and hospital assistants.

8. Low-cost forms of merchandising. During the Depression of the 1930s, the so-called dime stores did a booming business. Similar opportunities would undoubtedly emerge in any new depression. People still have to eat, clothe themselves, and take care of other basic needs; whoever can provide these at the lowest cost will find a market. Cooperatives, which utilize their members' time and skills, are likely to flourish.

This is not meant to be an exhaustive list of job opportunities under conditions of depression, but it provides a framework which the reader can use to evaluate his own situation. There will undoubtedly be opportunities in many other fields. It should be remembered that the competition for available jobs throughout the economy will be much more severe, that the income will be lower, and that life in general will be harder, though not without its satisfactions. Adversity has its own compensations. Perhaps the most positive factor that is likely to emerge in such an environment is a tendency for people to feel a closer rapport with their fellow men. Prosperity, particularly one that is based in large part on illusory inflation, tends to alienate people from each other, while adversity pulls them together. It has been said that morale in Great Britain was never higher than at the time of the German air attacks. Similarly, the adverse conditions of a depression are likely to bring out some very positive qualities among the American people.

Here are some of the fields that are likely to experience a severe contraction under depression conditions, and which should therefore be avoided by those in search of new jobs:

1. Banking. All banks will find their scope of operations greatly reduced in a depression environment. Quite a few of them may go out of business altogether. Investment banks are the most vulnerable, as people who have just lost the bulk of their investments are hardly in a mood to start on another round. The volume of business activity and private borrowing will be down to a fraction of its former level. Much of the time and energies of bankers will be spent on rescuing what they can from borrowers going through bankruptcy procedures.

2. Advertising, promotion, public relations, and the communications media. All of these areas will be cut back severely because the funds from advertisers will be lacking. Under conditions of depression, people purchase only absolute necessities. Advertising and promotion will fall on deaf ears, for people have neither the money nor the interest in things that are not absolutely essential. Necessities require little or no advertising.

3. Luxury-related activities. Art galleries, antique stores, luxury cars, expensive real estate, restaurants, travel, resorts, boats, and so on will find themselves with few customers. In fact, as part of the wave of bankruptcies, these will be among the categories that will be dumped on the market at any price in order to raise funds for meeting obligations. For those who have put their financial houses in order ahead of time, there will be many opportunities for picking up fine art and luxury buildings at unbelievably low prices. To illustrate this point, an acquaintance informed me that in 1936 he was offered four brownstone buildings on Central Park South, a prestigious section of New York City, for $36,000. These same buildings were sold about thirty years later for well over $1 million. Of course, in the 1930s one could have bought General Motors and Standard Oil of New Jersey stock for a fraction of their subsequent price. Fortunes can be built during depression times if one has the cash to take advantage of the opportunities. Very few are in that position.

4. All businesses that are highly leveraged in terms

of their financial structure. Debt is death under depression conditions. Any business that is heavily dependent on debt for its normal operations is bound to get into trouble during a depression. Virtually the whole field of real estate falls into this category. Shipping lines are extremely vulnerable. The same applies to airlines. Many utilities will be in serious financial trouble and may end up being taken over by various units of government.

5. With tongue in cheek, mention might be made of the possible effects such economic conditions would have on mate selection. Those men and women who want to have a reasonably solid economic foundation under their marriages will try to avoid mates with the wrong kind of profession or financial status. A poor prospect would be an investment banker with a luxury cooperative apartment, a yacht, and a heavy load of debt. He or she will most likely be wiped out in a crash. On the other hand, an ideal prospect would be a lawyer specializing in bankruptcy with all of his or her savings in U.S. Treasury bills. Such a person will probably end up with the banker's possessions and still have plenty left to buy real estate and stocks at bargain-basement prices.

It should be emphasized once again that inflation is only one factor in the decision-making process concerning investments, life-styles, and occupational choices. The fact that inflation should play such a role at all in affecting our lives is a sad commentary on the financial irresponsibility of the federal government, which is the sole cause of the problem. Top priority should therefore be given by all responsible citizens to taking an active part in the selection of proper candidates for office and the implementation of policies that will bring inflation under control as soon as possible.

INTO THE LION'S DEN

Anyone trying to convince the Washington bureaucracy that its ideas and procedures are unsound will soon discover how frustrating such a task can be. Bureaucrats have little interest in new ideas, particularly if they challenge the status quo or their power position. They will try to throw you off the track by telling you that any change from the established system would cause havoc, that another department has jurisdiction, that they are following orders, and so on. A commonsense approach to problem solving is virtually impossible under these circumstances.

    The understanding of economic affairs by government officials is limited, not only because of their inadequate knowledge of the subject matter, but also because of their power position. Governments have the power and resources to persist in policies that are clearly mistaken and counterproductive. There seems to be an inverse relationship between intelligence and power. In the private sector, power is limited and intelligence is essential for survival. In contrast, governments have virtually unlimited power and have much less need for intelligence. Even economists working for the government tend to lose whatever spark of creativity they might have had previously. They often seem to find it safest to play the game in accordance with the basic rule of bureaucracy: Don't rock the boat. Economists are hired to buttress the bureaucracy's position, not to challenge it. They soon learn to adjust to this reality or they lose their position.

People in governments tend to confuse their ability to impose their will on the public with proof of success and validity. For example, the very fact that they can get away with the inflation swindle proves to them that it must be the right policy. They are not motivated to examine their underlying premises or the ramifications of their actions. Their so-called success reflects the power dimension, not the legitimacy of their activity.

Because of these dynamics, government officials generally are not aware of the fact that the sole responsibility for causing inflation rests with them. As the effects of their financial manipulations permeate the economy, the private sector is blamed for anything that might go wrong, including inflation. It is a classic example of blaming the victim for the crime.

To get a clearer picture of how bureaucrats might respond to inquiries concerning their role in inflation, let us construct a hypothetical meeting between representatives of the Federal Reserve and myself.

I: Gentlemen, I have reached the conclusion that the Federal Reserve's policy of using fiat funds for converting government debts into new reserve assets of the banking system is at the core of the inflation problem.

FR: You are quite mistaken. When we purchase government securities in the open market, we do so to help stabilize the economy and to provide funds necessary for growth and full employment.

I: The record would indicate that your policies have achieved neither solid growth nor full employment. The economy has been sluggish for the past several years and unemployment rates approaching 8 percent are hardly inspiring.

FR: Insofar as financial policies can help the economy, we have done everything possible. Of course, we also try to prevent high levels of inflation. The unemployment may be the unfortunate but necessary price to pay for avoiding higher inflation rates.

I: I believe you are twisting cause and effect around. Full employment does not cause inflation; by the same token, unemployment does not reduce inflation. You people seem to be completely blind to the reality that it is your creation of fiat money that causes the problem, not the people who are doing an honest day's work to earn their livelihood.

FR: Our economists tell us that full employment can indeed cause inflation. We must be prepared to trade off inflation against unemployment. This is a most complex matter, to which we devote much time and study. As to your remarks about fiat money, we can only reiterate that without these funds the economy could go into a tailspin and experience a recession of a magnitude not seen since the 1930s.

I: In other words, after forty years of manipulating the economy you have created such a weak and dependent entity that any changes in your operations would be catastrophic.

FR: We feel there is nothing wrong with our continuing operations that seem to have worked reasonably well over the past several decades. We have had our ups and downs, but without us things would have been far worse.

I: The United States experienced its biggest and most solid growth during its first hundred and fifty years. There was no chronic inflation; in fact, had George Washington returned to us in 1940, he would have found that the purchasing power of his savings had remained intact since 1790. In contrast, ever since the Federal Reserve started its money-supply manipulations on a massive scale during World War II, we have experienced chronic inflation.

FR: The earlier times were simpler. The economy had its vacillations in those days, too. In fact, the Great Depression of the 1930s was the very reason we started to take measures to inflate (embarrassed cough)—I mean to increase the money supply. The country was flat on its back and the only way we could get it moving was to make money freely available.

I: The evidence is strong that your policies did not really work during the 1930s; they did not restore normal economic activity or significantly reduce unemployment. The outbreak of the war quickly restored full economic activity and employment. Under those conditions, even John Maynard Keynes, your big hero, recommended policies designed to mop up extra funds and avoid inflationary monetary procedures. You apparently listened to him only so long as it suited your purposes.

FR: We never said that Keynes was our hero. He had some good ideas in the 1930s, but toward the end of his life he seemed to have lost his enthusiasm for what we consider to be the right policies.

I: It seems more likely that Keynes recognized the fact that the policies he recommended in the 1930s were not applicable to the realities of the 1940s. Did that ever occur to you?

FR: We are not here to analyze Keynes. It is our considered opinion that the policies followed by the Federal Reserve in the past forty years have worked reasonably well, and we see no reason to change them.

I: When you claim that your policies worked well, you are in effect saying that the creation of some $100 billion of counterfeit-like funds, leveraged to an estimated $700 billion via the banking system, had a significant impact on the economy. No one can deny that. However, the main beneficiary of this dubious operation was the federal government, not the economy. For example, flooding the

158

economy with fiat money has pushed interest rates down. As the largest single borrower, the government is the major beneficiary of such low interest rates.

FR: We do not consider our creation of new money "counterfeiting" as you call it. After all, we have the legal right to issue such funds, while counterfeiters are engaged in illegal acts. As to interest rates, we regard reasonable levels as essential for a growing economy. If we did not control interest rates, economic progress would quickly come to a stop.

I: Counterfeiting may be too strong a term for your activities, but unfortunately the effect is the same as if it were counterfeiting. It is money that is created out of thin air without any real value behind it. You create by a stroke of the pen what everybody else has to work for. Getting back to interest rates, what you seem to overlook is the fact that these artificially depressed interest rates cause grievous losses to all creditors of the government. I have prepared a study which shows that those who purchased government securities during the past thirty-six years lost money in virtually every year.

FR: We do not set the interest rates on government securities. That is the province of the U.S. Treasury. Furthermore, nobody forces anyone to purchase government securities. Finally, we hold close to $100 billion of such securities, and we don't complain about interest rates.

I: If I may be blunt about this, I believe you are trying to pass the buck. I know that you and the Treasury work closely together, particularly on matters relating to government debt issues and financing programs. If one examines the record, one finds that you have always followed policies that have accommodated the Treasury's trips to the market for funds at the best possible rates. You have quite obviously favored the Treasury over its creditors. The purchase of government securities is not as free a matter as you imply. For example, government trust funds, such as the Social Security Administration, have no choice but to purchase government securities. This puts them in the difficult position of having income that is below inflation rates but having to pay its obligations on a basis that reflects such rates. As a result, Social Security is periodically forced to increase its levies, lest it go bankrupt. This is just one example of the distortions caused by your policies. Finally, your comments about your own holdings of government securities are grossly misleading. You acquired those securities with fiat funds; in actuality, you paid nothing for them. Furthermore, you are not a true creditor of the Treasury; you are merely another branch of the same government. To avoid any confusion about your government securities portfolio, you ought to hand it over to the Treasury and let them retire it. Consider it a gift from the American people to their Treasury.

FR: The Social Security operation is a separate problem, with which we have no direct concern. We might only comment that by having put their funds into government securities, at least they know for sure that the principal is safe. Whatever losses they might suffer on interest rates not reflecting inflation rates will undoubtedly be rectified by Congress as problems arise. Your suggestion for turning over our holdings of government securities to the Treasury is not as simple as you appear to think. Our member banks have a certain stake in our operations; we cannot simply turn assets over to another agency without appropriate procedures. To be quite frank, we have not checked into the matter, and we see no reason to do so unless Congress or the President demand such action. It would obviously greatly reduce our stature and power, for these holdings represent some 80 percent of our total assets. You people outside the government don't seem to understand the way Washington works. Would you give up 80 percent of your power, however you measure it, without a fight?

I: Quite frankly, my concern is not with who has the most power in the various bureaucracies, but with what we can do to bring inflation under control and how we can avoid further mischief. I believe these $100 billion of government securities in your portfolio may be misused in the future, and your comments do not reassure me. But let us return to the subject of the government's gains from inflation. In addition to artificially low interest rates, the government also benefits from inflation because it can repay debts with depreciated dollars; it increases its income tax receipts disproportionately because of escalating tax rates; and it taxes the inflation adjustment in interest rates. Altogether, these benefits aggregate tens of billions of dollars yearly. They give the government a strong incentive to continue inflationary policies. Furthermore, the knowledge by Congress that these dynamics are at work is a major contributor to the financial irresponsibility that characterizes our government. In effect, the Federal Reserve's monetary policies have become a substitute for constitutional budget and tax procedures.

FR: We have nothing to do with income taxes; you ought to address those comments to the Treasury. As to the Congress, we have periodically pointed out to them that they ought to move in the direction of fiscal responsibility and budget balance in times of full employment. We do not agree that our procedures have become a substitute for congressional action on taxes or budgets. Insofar as our monetary policies have an effect on other branches of the government, they are not intended as violations of constitutional provisions. We have of course certain obligations to the rest of the government, but in general we have expressed ourselves time and again as favoring governmental responsibility and the avoidance of policies that lead to increased inflation. As you may know, we are often criticized by members of Congress and others for not doing enough to help the economy. If we followed the advice of some of our critics, we would probably have chronic double-digit inflation.

I: It is true that you have talked a good game, but your actions have generally leaned in the direction of accommodating the politicians and bureaucrats who want to increase the flow of fiat funds to further their goals. In any case, the cumulative effect of your monetary policies, resulting in an estimated $700 billion of fiat funds being infused into the economy, fully accounts for the chronic inflation and many other problems that confront us today. I believe your actions, however well-intentioned, are counterproductive for the economy, unfair to all savers, taxpayers, and the creditors of the government, and unconstitutional as well, for they deprive people of their property on a massive scale without due process of law.

FR: We disagree with you on all counts. We believe we are helping the economy. The proof of this will be seen if our operations are ever discontinued; we predict disaster. We will do everything we can to safeguard savings from loss due to bank failures. We do not believe that our policies are as directly responsible for inflation as you claim. We reject the notion that we are depriving people of their property in an unconstitutional fashion, for we are not gaining anything for ourselves from this procedure. If your claims have any substance, and we don't say they have, you ought to talk to the Treasury.

I: I do not doubt that you have good intentions, but I am more concerned about the results. I am aware of the fact that other government agencies, notably the Treasury, are involved in the overall picture. As a concerned citizen, I want to see a systematic effort to root out the inflation threat from all facets of the government. I started with you because your role is the most direct and in many respects the most important. By the way, you did gain substantial benefits from your inflationary policies. Concretely, you hold almost $100 billion of government securities which you acquired for nothing. They belong to the American people and ought to be returned to them, by letting the Treasury retire them from the debt. Also, you have gained enormous power in Washington and over the economy. As to the concrete problem of protecting savers, the big problem today is not bank failures but inflation. In 1975 alone savers lost more money from inflation than they did from all the bank failures since the 1930s. If you want to do something meaningful for the savers, why don't you remove ceilings from interest rates that member banks can pay on savings deposits? This at least would be a step in the direction of providing a better return—one that would reflect more of the inflationary realities.

FR: This is a most complex subject. We recognize that savers are being hurt by inflation. At the same time, we feel that we cannot allow interest rates to fluctuate without some controls, lest mortgage markets become upset. Furthermore, our open market operations might be made more difficult if there were no ceiling on interest rates paid by banks.

I: This is precisely the point I am trying to make. Your policies have deliberately caused savers and purchasers of government securities enormous losses, just so that you could manipulate the economy in what you considered to be the appropriate fashion. You have in effect penalized the savers of this country for the benefit of the profligate spenders, notably the government itself.

FR: Here you are accusing us of being the guilty party again. We told you before and we reiterate that we have no intention of either causing inflation or deliberately harming anyone's interests. Our role is much more limited than you seem to think.

I: Intentions are quite irrelevant; what counts are the results that stem from your actions. These are indeed of great significance and in my opinion have caused a great deal of harm to the economy, to savers, taxpayers, and to the creditors of the government.

After this hypothetical exchange with the Federal Reserve, I might hold a similar imaginary meeting with officials of the U.S. Treasury.

I: Gentlemen, I just left the Federal Reserve, where we discussed the problem of inflation. A number of issues came up which had best be clarified with you. My studies indicate that investors in government securities lost money in virtually all years since 1940 because of a combination of inflation and low interest rates.

UST: We do not set the interest rates; they are determined by the market.

I: That is only true if you go by externals. What happened is that during the past thirty-six years the Federal Reserve converted almost $100 billion in government securities into new reserve assets of the banking system, thus generating an estimated $700 billion of new fiat funds. The latter of course depressed interest rates and also caused the inflation. The U.S. Treasury was the major beneficiary of this operation.

UST: We had nothing to do with Federal Reserve policy. We merely took advantage of the best available opportunities for financing our loans at the lowest costs.

I: Actually, the relationship between the Treasury and the Federal Reserve is very close; to say that you have nothing to do with Federal Reserve policy is a rather specious argument. From all indications, the Federal Reserve facilitates your borrowing operations and helps you achieve these low costs. You are in effect taking advantage of a procedure that comes pretty close to legalized counterfeiting to defraud your creditors.

UST: We resent the implications of that remark. We are doing no counterfeiting, nor does the Federal Reserve. The latter is authorized by Congress to maintain an elastic money supply to facilitate economic growth. That is quite different from counterfeiting, which is an illegal procedure.

I: I called the Federal Reserve's procedure "legalized counterfeiting" to acknowledge the difference you stated. However, in terms of what happens to your creditors, the effect is the same. They suffer just as much from legalized counterfeiting as from the illegal variety. In fact, because of the enormous scope, the legalized form is far more devastating than all the illegal counterfeiting in history put together. In any case, it seems wrong to me that the Treasury should take advantage of such a dubious procedure for its own gain. The purchasers of government securities deserve fairer treatment. I have made a proposal that the government issue inflation-proof bonds, which would provide protection against inflation plus a very modest interest payment.

UST: The Treasury has always opposed issuing bonds with cost-of-living escalator clauses and we see no reason to change that policy. If we sold such bonds, our interest costs might skyrocket and our budget would become even more unbalanced than it is. Furthermore, such a procedure would constitute only a form of symptom treatment, for it would not stop inflation. We believe inflation should be tackled head-on.

I: I know that the Treasury has resisted the idea of inflation-proof bonds, but I feel that your position is mistaken. Just because you have done something wrong for the past forty years does not mean that you should persist in such a stand. My purpose in being here is to call your attention to new ways of looking at realities, not to justify what you have been doing all along. As to your argument that inflation-proofing might increase your interest costs, let us look at this matter objectively. You have practically forced your creditors to subsidize you for the past several decades. Do you believe that they can afford better than you the chronic losses they suffered on government securities? If the Treasury needs more funds to pay legitimate interest costs, then let it turn to the Congress for appropriation of such funds and not rely on money manipulations by the Federal Reserve to defraud your creditors. As to your comment that inflation-proofing would be mere symptom treatment and would not stop inflation, it would certainly make a lot of difference to all those purchasing government securities. This procedure would restore fairness to the relationship between borrowers and lenders, which is one of the prime prerequisites in the fight against inflation. Ever since the New Deal, the government's monetary policies have systematically benefited borrowers, notably itself, at the expense of creditors. This is a shameful policy and should be terminated as soon as possible. By the way, I don't quite understand what you mean by tackling inflation head-on.

UST: To take the last item first, we believe that inflation is caused by excessive wages and prices, not by government monetary policy. While there are various points of view on the subject, some of us feel that the way to stop inflation is to institute appropriate wage and price controls. As to getting Congress to appropriate more funds for debt servicing, this is not as easy as you might think. We are being constantly criticized by Congress for paying too much interest, because that drives up everybody else's interest costs. Congressmen feel that this interferes with the proper economic stimulation.

I: In my view, wage and price controls constitute symptom treatment, while curbing the Federal Reserve's fiat money operation represents a frontal attack. Wage earners and businessmen do not cause inflation; they merely respond to the inflationary realities created in Washington. When the wages of government employees are raised in line with inflation, you people are strangely silent about the supposed inflationary impact. In fact, I understand that your pensions, too, are inflation-proofed. If you want these benefits for yourselves, why do you want to blame your fellow citizens for demanding the same protection?

UST: We are not blaming anybody for trying to get the most he can. The point we were trying to make is that if Congress passed a law making everybody toe the line on wages and prices, no one would gain any advantages and inflation would be curbed.

I: It has not worked out that way. If you look at the record, wage and price controls work only on a temporary basis, and even then they create all kinds of distortions, misallocation of resources, black markets, and other problems. When controls are removed, all the pent-up price changes that were held back by the controls loom up at once and generate double-digit inflation. The most recent example of that was 1974. I believe that if Congress faced realities and curbed the powers of the Federal Reserve to issue fiat money at will, we would come much closer to a realistic solution to the inflation problem. Speaking of Congress, I sympathize with your difficulties in getting them to see the light, but your stance would be much stronger if you faced up to the reality that forcing creditors to accept chronic losses on their investments in U.S. government securities is untenable. Many politicians obviously live in a world of economic unreality. You, however, who have technical competence in this area ought to help in the process of confronting politicians with the facts. Unfortunately, you seem to have spent more of your energies trying to shield politicians from having to face economic realities. Unwittingly, you have allowed yourselves to become their tools in a process that is full of dangers to the whole economy.

UST: We try to have good relations with Congress, for they pass the legislation that is the basis for our operations. It may seem simple to you to stand up to Congress, but they hold the whip over us and we had better not alienate them.

I: It is a sad commentary on our government that in spite of the separation of powers, the actual dynamics are such that no one dares take a stand on behalf on what is right, lest he antagonize politicians or other bureaucrats. If we cannot rely on you fellows to protect investors, to whom shall we turn?

UST: We do not consider it our duty to look out for the investors. No one is forcing them to buy our securities. As the saying goes, *caveat emptor,* "let the buyer beware."

I: I believe that is good advice and I hope investors will take due note of it. Perhaps they ought to form protective committees, similar to those that have been set up in connection with some of the bond issues of unreliable foreign governments. A U.S. Government Bondholders Protective Committee might indeed be well worth trying. Thank you for the idea.

UST: Wait a minute, we did not say anything about that. You were the one who took off on that idea; all we said was "Let the buyer beware." We want to make very clear that the Treasury does not look with favor upon the establishment of any U.S. Bondholders Protective Committee. We hope you squelch that idea before anybody does anything about it. We have enough troubles as it is. To deal with organized bondholders would be one big headache for us that we would just as soon avoid.

I: Turning to something else, the Treasury benefits from inflation in another major way through escalating income tax rates. Moreover, the Internal Revenue Service, one of your divisions, taxes the inflation factor in interest rates. This could be considered a form of expropriation of property without due process of law. It seems to me that there should be a thorough overhaul of the tax structure to adjust for as many facets of inflation as possible.

UST: If we followed your suggestions, we would probably lose tens of billions of dollars yearly. Where would we get the funds to pay for all this? You worry about inflation; if we inflation-proofed our securities and our income tax laws, our deficits would reach astronomical levels.

I: That is precisely the point I am trying to make. The Treasury now gains tens of billions of dollars from inflation annually, which is in turn caused by the massive infusion of fiat funds into the economy by the Federal Reserve. The best way to stop inflation is to take away the government's incentive for causing it. As long as you have these enormous gains from inflation, you will not be strongly motivated to take the appropriate steps to bring inflation under control. At the same time, I am prepared to support realistic tax policies to make up for your reduced income from inflation.

UST: We would rather not change procedures from what they are now to relying on new taxes as you propose.

It is hard enough to get tax laws changed under normal circumstances; what you suggest is so different that it probably has no chance of passing. In any case, the Treasury opposes inflation-proofing income tax laws.

I: It may interest you to know that a recent Secretary of the Treasury, Mr. William E. Simon, apparently held a different position. In an interview with editors of *U.S. News & World Report*, dated March 10, 1975, he is quoted as saying: "People pay a higher portion of their real incomes in taxes as inflation pushes incomes into higher-rate brackets. As a result, the Government becomes the beneficiary of rampaging inflation. One possibility that intrigues me is the notion of indexing a portion of the tax system to compensate for this. Indexing could also act as a discipline on Government spending, and I'm in favor of anything that disciplines Government."

UST: Did he really say that? This is news to us. As far as we know, nothing concrete along these lines has ever been done here. In any case, it is unrealistic and would upset too many established policies and procedures. Once you open the door to indexing, there is no knowing where it might all lead.

I: I believe that former Secretary Simon deserves credit for his forthrightness and willingness to explore new ideas. You fellows should not be so fearful of change, particularly if present procedures are unfair, unsound, and counterproductive. After all, the Treasury should set an example of correct behavior. Profiteering from inflation at the expense of creditors and taxpayers is not worthy of the great traditions and lofty ideals that should motivate the Treasury.

UST: That is all fine and good, but we have the job of making ends meet, and believe me it is not easy. We are spending over $1 billion a day, we have to raise about $1 billion of new money each week and refinance another $5 billion, and everybody wants something else from us. Cities want to be bailed out from their debts, defense contractors plead for money to avoid bankruptcy, foreign governments beg for money to survive in power. Do they think there is no limit? We believe we are much too overextended as it is.

I: I can sympathize with your problems. In my opinion, your present predicament reflects the inflationary realities that prevail. While the Treasury has gained certain benefits from inflation, the demands made upon it by Congress and others have grown even more. If everybody realized that inflation is an illusory road to riches, that realistic limits must be set on our spending programs, we would all be in better shape. I have concerned myself with this problem for over six years and have written a book about the subject which contains specific solutions that I believe to be sound and practical. For example, your refinancing problems could be greatly simplified if you issued long-term inflation-proof bonds with low fixed-interest rates. If politicians, bureaucrats, and the people get a better understanding of what inflation is, how it is caused, and the grave threats it poses, a concentrated effort can be made to bring it under control.

CONCLUSION

Inflation is as different from normal economics as cancer is from normal cell growth. It is a form of financial self-destruction. By means of massive infusion of fiat funds, the government has created a topsy-turvy situation in which all the rules of the game are turned around. Profligate behavior is rewarded, while prudence and self-discipline are penalized. The Golden Rule is replaced by naked aggression. People can no longer differentiate between right and wrong in financial matters. The government itself, while gaining immediate benefits from inflation, becomes increasingly embroiled in counterproductive behavior and jeopardizes its legitimacy. In the long run, no one gains from inflation except the enemies of free enterprise and democracy.

This phemonenon has been described most clearly by the father of economic theory, Adam Smith. In his opus, *Wealth of Nations*, Book V, Chapter 3, "Of Public Debt," he notes that governments throughout the ages have ma-

nipulated currencies for their own ulterior purposes when
they found themselves heavily in debt. These manipulations not only defrauded their creditors, but had devastating effects for the whole economy, often leaving it in
shambles. He called this procedure a "disguised form of
bankruptcy," which is far worse than normal bankruptcy
ɔcause it knows no limits. All politicians, bureaucrats,
nd concerned citizens should read this chapter to gain
an appropriate perspective on the danger facing us.

How could such a situation arise in a democratic
government, with all of its checks and balances? The
policies that generated inflation were initiated in the 1930s
as measures to fight the Depression. They were institutionalized and developed a life of their own. Moreover,
in the short run, irresponsible financial actions provide
political advantages, as they give the illusion of obtaining
something for nothing. In trying to legislate the good life
for everybody in the United States and all over the world,
our government has managed to undermine the monetary
system.

The inability of money to act as a stable standard of
value for long-term financial transactions has facilitated the
government's irresponsibility. If the government knew
that its loans would have to be paid for in full with the
purchasing power intact, the incentive to get something for
nothing at the expense of creditors would be removed. This
reality greatly strengthens the case for the procedures recommended by Alfred Marshall to protect purchasing
power.

Politicians and government officials will protest
that they do not want inflation. This is essentially true as
far as it goes. Nobody wants inflation, but most people
involved with running our government want those things
that can be obtained only through inflation. If the government were run along financially responsible lines, then all
of its spending programs would sooner or later have to be
paid for with taxes. The American people, who are already
among the most highly taxed in the world, would hardly be

in the mood for allowing politicians to increase these taxes indefinitely. Inflation bypasses popular consent to tax increases. It is the ultimate form of taxation without representation.

Since the institutional framework has failed to protect the people from this diabolical threat, it is imperative that they take the necessary steps to restore soundness to government. The first prerequisite to a solution is to know the unvarnished truth. Those who have read this book will, I hope, be well on the way to understanding the realities involved. Next there should follow active participation in the political process. The people should not underestimate their political power, if it is exerted with dedication to a just cause. Throughout history this nation has been moved by highly motivated individuals fighting for ideas whose time had come.

Taking the appropriate steps to conquer inflation will require imagination, persistence, and patience. Policies and procedures that have been taken for granted during the past four decades will have to be modified, eliminated, or even reversed. Much confusion can be avoided if we substitute the words "disguised bankruptcy" for the term "inflation." The procedure for dealing with inflation is basically identical with that for dealing with bankruptcy. This involves preservation of existing assets, the avoidance of new profligacies, and a systematic program of debt repayment. This should be combined with the restoration of sound currency through inflation-proofing procedures.

Lest I give the wrong impression, it should be emphasized that the basic strength of the United States remains formidable, despite forty years of financial mismanagement by the government. Our hard-working people are still growing more food, manufacturing more goods, and generating more wealth than any other country in the world. If we tackle the problem of inflation as suggested here, it will be a sign of our people's strength and proof of the viability of our political and economic institutions.

While this book has focused on chronic inflation as

manifested in the United States, the pattern is essentially the same in all countries. Any government that lives chronically beyond its means and piles up large deficits and debts will be tempted to generate inflation as a means of dealing with its profligacy. The particular mechanisms involved may vary, but in every case the purchasing power of currency will be reduced by governmental action. If unchecked, this process will ultimately destroy faith in the currency and cause a breakdown of the economic system, which is generally followed by political turmoil and the threat of totalitarianism. It is therefore imperative that all those who value their freedom and political heritage take an active part in bringing inflation under control by appropriate policies as soon as possible.

I should like to end this book with a plea for conciliation toward those who have wronged us. Our objective of an inflation-free economy can be accomplished more readily if we forgive past transgressions by the political and governmental establishment in return for wholehearted commitment to the correct approaches for bringing the problem under control. It is not our purpose to tear society apart, but to heal wounds and get on with a sound program without further delay.

EPILOGUE: A PERSONAL NOTE ON INFLATION

My active involvement in the battle against inflation started in 1970. Having placed some of my savings into U.S. government securities, I discovered that inflation, combined with taxes, forced me to accept a negative yield. In other words, by lending my money to the U.S. government I ended up with a loss of capital. By the same token, my loss was the government's gain. At first I thought that this might be an accidental occurrence, but when I checked the yields of government securities since 1940 I found out that interest rates were almost always inadequate to protect investors from loss of capital due to inflation and taxes. I was very puzzled by this, for I could not believe that the U.S. government would deliberately defraud its creditors.

I set to work developing a procedure that would rectify this error. It occured to me that the basic solution to the problem was to link the yield to the rate of inflation. The inflation rate should be kept separate from interest rates; since it constituted a loss of capital, it should not be taxed. If the government was willing to issue such inflation-proof securities, investors could accept a very low interest rate. In fact, on the basis of historical experience, *any* assured positive interest rate would have been a gain for investors. The latter could even agree to have the payment of the inflation adjustment deferred until the maturity date of the security, to provide the government with additional time and incentive to bring inflation under control.

I prepared a brief memorandum spelling out these ideas. The logic and fairness of my analysis were so self-evident to me that I felt it my duty as a citizen to make my findings available to our policy makers in Washington. In addition, I sent copies to some of my business friends. One of the latter, Mr. R. Hugh Uhlmann, chairman of the Standard Milling Company of Kansas City, Missouri, sent me a letter dated April 26, 1971, which turned out to be prophetic:

This morning I read with interest your proposal for an inflation proof U.S. Government bond. This is indeed a startling idea, one that is so sensible that I am afraid it has no possibility of adoption. On the other hand, if people like you will continue to have these ideas, perhaps something can be done along the lines you suggest. At any rate, it was a brilliant and provocative thought.

Mr. Uhlmann was right; the authorities in Washington were not moved to act on the basis of my logic. The U.S. Treasury, which is the agency most directly involved in issuing government bonds, summed up its position with this statement: "The Treasury has long been opposed to the concept of indexed securities" (letter dated March 31, 1971). The Federal Reserve noted that it had no jurisdiction in this matter (April 12, 1971). I made a trip to Washington to meet with a variety of officials about the issue. One of the economists on the Joint Economic Committee of Congress expressed sufficient interest in my ideas to arrange for me to meet a number of people who would help me attain a more realistic picture of the obstacles involved in getting anything done in Washington. One bureaucrat told me that he approved of inflation protection for government employee wages and pensions, but saw no reason to support such a policy with regard to the government's creditors. In effect he held the view, which is undoubtedly widespread among bureaucrats, that the government exists primarily for the benefit of its employees. The assistant to an important legislator on the Senate Banking Committee—a person of an obviously liberal persuasion—noted that if these bonds were restricted to purchase by union pension funds he might support the idea. I noted that I had no objection to union pension funds purchasing such bonds, but that the approach should not be restricted in that fashion. Altogether, the trip was enlightening but not productive of any meaningful results.

I made one more attempt to get my ideas across to the government. In the late spring of 1971, while traveling in Europe, I learned that Secretary of the Treasury Connally and Undersecretary for Monetary Affairs Volcker would attend the International Banking Conference in Munich. I managed to interview both men there. They were polite but basically reiterated the position already stated in letters from the Treasury—namely, that the latter was opposed to the issuance of inflation-proof bonds. Mr. Connally noted that he felt we should take more direct action against inflation, such as wage and price controls. These were instituted in August 1971. Subsequent events proved that this so-called direct action did not stop inflation. For the sake of historical accuracy it should be emphasized that Mr. Connally and Mr. Volcker did not originate the Treasury's opposition to inflation-proof bonds, nor were they the last to hold this view. The U.S. Treasury has unfortunately institutionalized this position, which I believe to be untenable on moral and constitutional grounds.

These experiences with government officials left me with a sense of frustration. I knew that my analysis was

177

correct and that the Treasury's position was wrong. However, mere logic was not going to convince the powers in Washington to change their ways. I decided to expand my investigations and to bide my time until an appropriate opportunity arose for further action.

The rate of inflation exceeded 6 percent in 1973 and jumped to 11 percent in 1974. I felt that the time was propitious for me to make my views known to a wider audience. I prepared an article entitled "Disguised Bankruptcy," which was published in *Barron's* on October 28, 1974. In this article I showed how inflation undermines the savings function and rewards the profligate spenders, notably the government, at the expense of the savers. The article was well received.

In January 1975 the government announced that it would have to engage in the biggest peacetime borrowing program in history. Deficits for 1975 and 1976 were estimated to aggregate some $100 billion. As a student of Adam Smith, I knew that increases in government debt of that magnitude would spell further inflation. I sat down and prepared an article entitled "Inflation-Proofing the U.S. Debt," which was published by *The Wall Street Journal* on February 28, 1975. It was an elaboration upon the original memorandum that I had sent to government officials in 1971. Readers from all over the United States responded favorably to this article, and Senator James Buckley of New York placed it in the Congressional Record of March 13, 1975. One of the most gracious letters came from Professor W. A. Paton of the Graduate School of Business Administration at the University of Michigan, a teacher well known for his textbooks on accounting:

I'm taking the liberty of writing a note primarily to congratulate you on your excellent piece in the Wall Street Journal.

I might add that I've been calling attention, to the best of my ability, in my classes, textbooks, and numerous articles, to the swindle being perpetrated by the government—in basic control of the monetary system—which borrows dollars and then proceeds to devalue, debase, the monetary unit.

Borrowing dollars and repaying in money units of the same amount but having less value is analogous to the neighbor who borrowed a farmer's milch cow and then tried to repay the loan by returning her young calf—on the ground that he borrowed "one head" and was returning "one head."

More power to you!.

These spontaneous comments by such fine people heartened me immensely and convinced me that the battle against inflation was not a total loss, even if the government ignored our calls for justice.

The most important breakthrough in my analysis of inflation occurred early in 1976. I was trying to discover possible statistical correlations between government debts and inflation rates. As I analyzed the debt figures, my curiosity was aroused by the fact that the Federal Reserve had increased its holdings of government securities from $2 billion to almost $100 billion between 1940 and 1975. I wondered where the Federal Reserve had gotten the money to pay for these securities. If the Federal Reserve, which is an integral part of the government, had that kind of money, why would the U.S. Treasury have to go out to borrow it? The whole thing did not make sense, until it occurred to me that the Federal Reserve used fiat money to acquire these securities. In other words, the Federal Reserve paid for its purchases by issuing checks that did not require any balance of money already in existence; these checks constituted newly created money. I decided to inquire into the actual procedures employed by the Federal Reserve in acquiring government securities.

I found that the Federal Reserve buys these securities on the open market. It pays with a check drawn on itself and presents it to the bank in exchange for the security. The bank now has newly created money at its dis-

179

posal. This new money will flow through the banking system until it has become multiplied by the denominator of the fractional reserve requirement. For example, if the reserve requirement is one-seventh of the total deposits, each newly created dollar will be converted into seven dollars in this fashion. According to my assessment of the situation, that seven-for-one ratio is probably fairly close to the current realities. This means in effect that the approximately $100 billion of Federal Reserve net purchases of government securities over the past thirty-six years have been converted by the banking system into some $700 billion of new fiat funds. I now felt I had the key to understanding how the government causes inflation. The magnitude of this conversion of government debt into new reserve assets of the banking system provided convincing evidence for the scope and persistence of the inflation that has plagued us since 1940.

    This insight into Federal Reserve operations also led to clarification of another basic issue—namely, the relationship between interest rates and inflation rates. I had wondered for some time how the government could year after year get away with paying interest rates that did not reflect the inflationary realities. In a truly free market environment investors would long ago have insisted on interest rates that fully reflect inflation rates plus a normal return on capital. However, since the New Deal days the Federal Reserve has not allowed normal interest rates to function, for the very procedure that infuses fiat funds into the economy on a leveraged basis also pushes interest rates down. In other words, the $700 billion of fiat funds compete with other money for loans and investments and drive down interest rates below those necessary to safeguard against inflation. Thus, interest rates cannot truly fulfill their function of impartiality between lenders and borrowers, nor can they lead to the optimum allocation of financial and economic resources. It is clear that a well-functioning free economic system is incompatible with chronic inflationary policies by the government.

All of the pieces of the puzzle now fell into place. Inflation was the inevitable outcome of self-serving financial procedures concocted by politicians and bureaucrats. While they rationalized that they were trying to help the economy, in actual fact they were adding to the problems of economic instability. They were undermining the monetary system, saddling their creditors and all savers with a disguised form of property expropriation, increasing taxes via the inflation route, and removing all external financial restraints from their own activities. It all added up to the biggest confidence game in history.

My discoveries affirmed the validity of Adam Smith's observation that governments heavily in debt use their control of the currency to defraud their creditors and in the process jeopardize the very existence of the free enterprise system. Ultimately, they even risk their people's freedom and independence, for history has shown that countries ravaged by chronic inflation often end up under totalitarian rule or even under foreign domination.

With the impetus provided by these insights, I now felt ready to tackle the problem of inflation afresh. I had a strong conviction that I was on the right track, and that I had an obligation to the American people to make these ideas available to them. These feelings sustained me in preparing the manuscript for this book.

One of my primary concerns was the moral dimension. I had known since 1970 that the government was benefiting from inflation by interest rates that did not reflect inflationary realities, by repaying maturing debts with depreciated dollars, and by increased income tax receipts due to escalating tax rates. If these gains had been due to accidental happenings, one could have excused the government's behavior. However, the evidence was now overwhelming that the government was the sole cause of the inflation. Therefore, its gains were morally wrong. If an individual engaged in similar behavior, he would be accused of fraud. I happen to believe that the same moral rules apply to governments as to people. If anything, governments should behave with greater respect for the moral code than individuals, for their behavior affects everybody else. I reached the conclusion that the government's inflationary policies constituted a swindle. The title for this book was a logical outgrowth of this interpretation.

The constitutional aspects of the problem also intrigued me. When one studies the U.S. Constitution and the background of events leading up to it, one finds that the founders of this country were very much concerned with the issue of safeguarding the people against tyranny and immoral behavior by the government. The religious injunction "Thou shalt not steal" was translated into secular terms: "No person shall be deprived of property, without due process of law" (Amendment V). Inflation takes away property on a massive scale and transfers it to the government without due process of law. As I understand the Constitution, it takes precedence over all administrative actions and even over laws of the Congress. The only way in which inflation could be made legitimate would be to pass a constitutional amendment to that effect. That has obviously not been done, nor is it likely that the American people would approve such an amendment.

If inflation is both immoral and unconstitutional, can it be justified on grounds of necessity? The government may claim that inflationary procedures were necessary to cope with the emergency conditions prevailing during the 1930s. Without going into the merits of this assertion, the question may be raised why these procedures were continued long after the emergency was over. An objective analysis of the facts indicates that this country's affairs could have been handled without perpetuating the inflation swindle. The propensity of bureaucracies and politicians to hold on to power is apparently greater than their concern with legitimacy of function or relevance to current realities. This blind drive for power leads to self-defeating, neurotic behavior which benefits no one.

In dealing with government bureaucrats, one must be aware of the fact that their perspective is limited and self-serving. They will generally provide explanations for their actions that attest to their good intentions and apparent logic. For example, when I inquired at the Federal Reserve about their open market operations in relation to interest rates, they tried to impress upon me that their sole focus was on the federal funds rate—the interest banks pay for funds they borrow from other banks, usually for one business day. If the Federal Reserve wants the federal funds rate to go down, it purchases government securities in the open market and pays for them with newly created fiat money, thus adding to bank reserves. The bureaucrats conveniently overlook the fact that this procedure affects all interest rates, not just federal funds rates. Moreover, the record clearly shows that the overall impact of Federal Reserve open market operations over the past four decades has been an enormous increase in fiat funds, chronic inflation, and an artificial lowering of all interest rates. The biblical injunction "By their fruits ye shall know them" is good advice to all those seeking the truth about government activities.

Philosophers, prophets, and moralists throughout history have dealt with the problem of governments that have abused their powers. In the Judeo-Christian tradition, these moral judgments were generally combined with a plea to forgive those who had done wrong, provided they mended their ways. I believe this procedure is applicable to the inflation swindle.

GLOSSARY

Bankruptcy: a condition characterized by the inability to repay debts in full, because the liabilities (amounts owed) exceed the assets. Legally, a bankrupt is an individual or corporate debtor who is judged insolvent by a court. Anyone chronically living beyond his means risks this condition.

Consumer Price Index: an index of the prices paid for goods and services by average wage earners living in urban areas, making up an estimated 45 percent of the U.S. population. This index is prepared by the Bureau of Labor Statistics.

Contingent liabilities: financial commitments that could be transformed into actual obligations in case of adverse developments. For example, the U.S. government's guarantees of mortgages would become actual obligations if the mortgagees fail to pay.

185

Cost-of-living index: an index of prices for goods and services making up the general cost of living. The Consumer Price Index is a specific example.

Counterfeiting: the illegal practice of creating imitation money with the intent to use it as currency. This practice is prohibited by all governments.

Credit rating: an assessment of the factors that determine the financial soundness of a borrower. For example, a person or corporation with a strong financial position, good income prospects, and a low level of indebtedness in relation to total net worth is given a high credit rating. In contrast, an entity with a weak financial position, poor income prospects, and a high level of debt in relation to net worth gets a low credit rating.

Debt monetizing: the procedure whereby the Federal Reserve issues new fiat money to pay for government debt obligations. This new money in effect replaces the debt.

Depreciation: the cost of capital goods, such as machinery and equipment, can be written off over their lives for tax purposes. For example, if a machine tool costs $1 million and has a normal life of ten years, the owner can depreciate it at the rate of $100,000 a year. This procedure does not take account of the realities in a chronic inflationary environment. For example, as a result of inflation the cost of the new tool to be purchased at the end of the ten years may have increased to $2 million. The depreciation fund will therefore be short $1 million. This pattern weakens the financial position of the private sector of the economy.

Easy-money policies: the procedure whereby the Federal Reserve infuses fiat funds into the banking system in order to make money and credit readily available at interest rates that do not reflect the inflationary realities.

Federal Reserve System: the central banking system of the United States, consisting of twelve Federal Reserve Banks and supervised by the Federal Reserve Board, whose members are appointed by the President.

Fiat money: currency whose value is determined by the command of the ruler. This applies to all paper money not redeemable into gold or silver at stipulated rates. By law, in the United States only the Federal Reserve can create new money by fiat.

FIFO method of accounting: the costs of sales are determined on the basis of "first in, first out" under this procedure. Chronic inflationary conditions penalize a company that employs this method, for the goods purchased first usually have the lowest cost and thus result in high profits subject to taxes. Because these goods have to be replaced with those of higher cost, the net effect is a drain on the financial resources of the corporation.

Fractional reserve basis: see *Reserve ratio.*

General price level: the average price of all goods and services. Inflation is characterized by a rising trend in the general price level.

Government: unless otherwise specified, the term "government" as used in this book refers to the federal government of the United States.

Income tax: an annual levy on the income of U.S. citizens and corporation. The tax rate escalates upward as the income increases. For example, in 1976 an individual earning between $20,000 and $22,000 had to pay 38 percent tax on the income above $20,000. On income above $100,000, the tax rate is 70 percent. These figures refer only to the federal income tax. In addition, many states and cities also levy income taxes whose rates escalate upward. Thus, residents of New York City have to pay taxes to the federal government, the state, and the city.

Indexing: see *Inflation-proofing.*

Inflation-proofing: protecting savings and other fixed-income investments from inflation by linking them to an objective standard reflecting changes in purchasing power, such as the Consumer Price Index. For example, if the Consumer Price Index goes up by 10 percent in a given year, inflation-proofed instruments would automatically go up by the same amount. This would keep their purchasing power intact.

Negative yield: when the return from savings is less than the rate of inflation and taxes. The result is loss of capital.

New reserve assets: payments received by banks from the Federal Reserve in the form of checks that represent newly created fiat money. Banks use these funds to generate new loans and investments in line with the denominator (the portion of the fraction written below the line) of their average reserve requirements. For example, if these requirements are one-tenth (10 percent) of deposits, then the banks can lend out or invest $10 for each $1 created by the Federal Reserve. It should be noted that only the Federal Reserve can create new reserve assets, because it alone has the power to issue new money. All other domestic banking transactions merely shift funds from one bank to another without affecting the total reserves of the banking system.

Purchasing power: the goods and services that can

be purchased with a given amount of money. Inflation is reflected in loss of purchasing power of the currency. For example, if it now takes $2 to pay for goods and services that formerly cost $1, the purchasing power of the dollar has been cut in half.

Real terms: how purchasing power is affected by inflation.

Reserve assets: cash that a bank must keep in its vaults and/or with the Federal Reserve as a backing for its deposits. The amounts involved depend on the size of the bank's total deposits. See *Reserve requirements* for further details.

Reserve ratio: the ratio between funds held in reserve and total deposits. For example, if a bank keeps $1 million in reserves and has deposits of $10 million, the reserve ratio is one to ten. Since the relationship between deposits and reserves is the key to understanding how the banking system works, the following illustration may be helpful.

Imagine an independent country with its own currency and a single bank. It has one thousand inhabitants, each of whom has inherited $1,000 and the full amount is deposited in the bank. Deposits at the bank now total $1 million. The bank seeks to convert these deposits into earning assets in the form of loans and investments. The bank's officers realize that they must keep some reserves for demands by depositors; let us assume the amount is fixed at 10 percent. As a result, the bank keeps $100,000 in its vaults and lends out or invests $900,000. What happens to this $900,000? It is spent or invested by the recipients of the bank's loans or investments. Because in this hypothetical case there is only one bank, the full $900,000 eventually comes back to this bank in the form of deposits. The cycle is now repeated, with $90,000 (10 percent) added to reserves and $810,000 available for loans and investments. Ultimately, the whole $1 million originally deposited end up as reserves for deposits now aggregating $10 million.

What would happen if the bank kept reserves larger than the $1 million? It would lose income because of excess reserves. On the other hand, if more than $1 million were demanded by depositors at once, the bank would have to sell off investments and/or close out loans to meet the demand. Under extreme circumstances, this could lead to the demise of the bank, for there is a limit to how much money it can raise on short notice. If a second bank opened for business and attracted funds away from the first one, the figures cited would not be changed as long as both banks maintained the same reserve ratios.

Reserve requirements: the ratio of funds to deposits that banks have to keep in their vaults. This ratio varies with the size of the bank's deposits. The Federal Reserve stipulates what these ratios must be. Changes in reserve requirements are used by the Federal Reserve to influence monetary conditions. If the Federal Reserve wants to make money and credit easier to obtain, it lowers reserve requirements; if a tightening of monetary conditions is desired, the reserve requirements are raised. As of December 20, 1976, reserve requirements were as follows: 7 percent for banks with net demand deposits of $2 million or less; 9½ percent for banks with net demand deposits of $2–10 million; 11¾ percent for banks with net demand deposits of $10–100 million; 12¾ percent for banks with net demand deposits of $100–400 million; and 16¼ percent for banks with net demand deposits of over $400 million.

"Unseen hand of the market": the phrase used by Adam Smith to explain how demand and supply for goods and services are brought into balance at optimum prices through free competition in the market.

Wealth: accumulated funds and the material resources they represent. If the funds lose purchasing power through inflation, wealth is reduced.